PARENTING CHILDREN WITH MENTAL HEALTH CHALLENGES

PARENTING CHILDREN WITH MENTAL HEALTH CHALLENGES

A Guide to Life with Emotionally Complex Kids

DEBORAH VLOCK

ROWMAN & LITTLEFIELD
Lanham • Boulder • New York • London

Published by Rowman & Littlefield
An imprint of The Rowman & Littlefield Publishing Group, Inc.
4501 Forbes Boulevard, Suite 200, Lanham, Maryland 20706
www.rowman.com

Unit A, Whitacre Mews, 26-34 Stannary Street, London SE11 4AB

British Library Cataloguing in Publication Information Available

Library of Congress Cataloging-in-Publication Data

Names: Vlock, Deborah, author.
Title: Parenting children with mental health challenges : a guide to life with
    emotionally complex kids / Deborah Vlock.
Description: Lanham : Rowman & Littlefield, [2018] | Includes bibliographical
    references and index.
Identifiers: LCCN 2018009447 (print) | LCCN 2018011042 (ebook) | ISBN
    9781538105252 (electronic) | ISBN 9781538105245 (cloth : alk. paper)
Subjects: LCSH: Parents of mentally ill children. | Mentally ill children. | Parent
    and child.
Classification: LCC RJ499 (ebook) | LCC RJ499 .V595 2018 (print) | DDC
    618.92/89—dc23
LC record available at https://lccn.loc.gov/2018009447

Printed in the United States of America

For J.D., A.G.V.D., and T.M.V.D.,
without whom there would be no us.

For Ruth and Richard Vlock,
who showed me how to be a good parent.

CONTENTS

ACKNOWLEDGMENTS

I wish there'd been no need for this book when I first began to wonder whether I should write it. I wish there were no need for it now. As my wishes on the matter are irrelevant, I eventually went ahead and wrote it. After all, maladies of the psyche will probably always exist while there are human beings on this earth. I'm grateful to have had the chance to offer encouragement and advice to some of the other human beings who know, or will come to know, what living with a mental illness feels like.

Inside these pages, my hand is waiting to clasp yours—much like other parents have extended a hand to me when, over the years, I've needed rescue from drowning. The wonderful kids and parents who chose to share their stories here, and the clinicians and other professionals who likewise came forward to proffer advice, have all done so because they want to help. Without their generous input, there's no way this book could have been written—certainly not in its current form.

A big shout-out to the millions of children and families, just here in the U.S. alone, facing down a mental illness. You wake up every day and continue the weary work of simply getting by till tomorrow. You know what the stab of loneliness, severe sleep deprivation, and being in a prolonged state of fight-or-flight arousal feels like. You've battled shape-shifting adversaries and been held hostage by psych meds you can't live with yet can't live without. Uncertainty is your baseline: never knowing what's coming tonight, tomorrow, next week. There's no one braver, in my estimation, than you!

To the parents and kids who offered up your stories for this book, so readers in search of comfort and solidarity might find a bit of both, thank you! Here's to you—and the dream of a future in which books like this one are obsolete.

A handful of outstanding mental health clinicians, advocates, and related professionals were good enough to share their knowledge with me. Jessica Reed, LICSW; Cynthia Moore; Anne Glowinski, MD; Leon Hammer, MD; and Kate Maffa, your expertise has made this book all the better.

Although my own life has been periodically challenged by illness and loss, my sleep disrupted by the ever-present potential for more of both, I must say, I won the family lottery. In "Lars" I've found a true partner—a loving husband and dad, willing to embark with me on this unexpected parenting detour, and to face together some hard truths about our own "unquiet minds" along the way. You are truly peerless at what you do and who you are: smart, funny, sweet, unflaggingly loyal, and a forever kind of guy.

"Saskia" and "Ben": you are my true north, my greater purpose, my shining examples of how to undertake the tricky work of *being good people in this world*, and do it right. Not perfectly, maybe, but with deep human feeling, sometimes human fallibility, and enough courage to be true to yourselves while striving to do right by others. I'm lucky to have learned from you guys what unconditional love—given and received—feels like. (It feels beautiful.)

My parents, Richard and Ruth Vlock, have probably read every damn thing I've written since I penned my first poem around the age of six. They pored tirelessly over every draft of every chapter of this book, with love and enthusiasm, and possibly a semiprivate, long-standing belief that I am the greatest living writer in the English language. (What—that's why parents were invented, no?)

My brother and sister-in-law, Rob Vlock and Joanne Southwell, both authors as well, have been my comrades in all varieties of artistic neurosis. I love you two. And I'll bet you twenty bucks it'll be one (or both) of you, among the three of us, who touches the writerly stars first. Go, go, go!

Anke Finger, rock-star professor and my bestie since we took ourselves way too seriously in graduate school, you have been a most cherished reader and friend for a long time. May we have many years to come of mutual beta reading. Oh . . . plus good coffee and German chocolate, always and forever.

A special thank-you to my amazing critique group, who feel like family after many years together. Readers, look sharp (now and in the future) for writings by Diana Renn, Patrick Gabridge, Eileen Donovan-Kranz, Rob Vlock, Ted Rooney, Gregory Lewis, Erin Cashman, and Julie Wu—each one an inimitable talent.

This book is only a "thing" because my agent extraordinaire, Janet Reid, is determined and loyal, sticking with me while I figured out what book I really needed to write. After one or two unsold novels, a couple of near misses, and some veiled threats that I was going to stop writing altogether, here we are. I'm lucky to have been a longtime partner in literary endeavors with you, Janet—and even better, to count you as a friend.

Suzanne Staszak-Silva, my editor at Rowman & Littlefield, was just the person to see the value in this book and acquire it. What can I say, Suzanne, except that without your trust, who knows whether this survival guide would ever have come to pass? I know you hope, as much as I do, that it will make a difference in many lives.

Last but far from least, there are a few people who mean the world to me, and whose basic presence in my life furthers many of the things I do. Thanks to Jessica, Emily, and Mark Axel; the King-Maranci family; the Zendzian family; the Donovan-Kranz crew; and Cynthia Moore, if not for whose dedicated friendship and advocacy, our family might have been lesser by one beloved person. Like the others mentioned here, Eve Golden and Ken Kronenberg spent many an anguished hour with us when life was nipping at our flanks something fierce. Without Eve's wise and gentle counsel, we would likely have lacked the courage to take the very first step—a residential school for Ben—that marked the end of a dire phase and the beginning of a hopeful, lovely one.

INTRODUCTION

Do we know each other?
Maybe not personally, but if you're . . .

- A parent
- Filled with love for a child you "can't live with, and can't live without"
- Functioning on two hours' sleep and sheer determination
- Willing to do whatever it takes to make things "right"—if only you can figure out what those things are, or whom to ask for the "twelve-steps to a cure" program
- Shocked and devastated to learn that there *is* no such list, any-where—not even in the hands of the most acclaimed mental health clinicians in the world

. . . then you may just be one of *us*: the many folks who are parenting kids with a showstopping psychiatric illness. If so, then yes, we're already acquainted—in spirit, if not in the flesh.

Welcome to the club, friend.

WHAT'S IN THIS BOOK, WHAT'S NOT, AND WHY YOU'LL WANT TO READ IT

You're the world's invisible superheroes, fighting for your hurting kids every day. You comfort, and cheer on, the ones who need you most. Your child may or may not (yet) have a concrete psychiatric diagnosis, but still, you do what you must, with a parent's instinct, and hope for the best.

You deserve a medal, or at least a lifetime supply of wine and chocolate, for trying and trying to help your kid, and never giving up. So why do you feel unacknowledged and alone?

I think I know why. The issue is partly a widespread silence among people living with mental health disorders. There's a lot of cultural stigma and public misinformation, which can make disclosure a risky business. In other words, you can feel unacknowledged and alone despite the statistical probability that you've got neighbors, and maybe even friends or family, who are dealing with similar challenges but are afraid or ashamed to speak out about it. And because you, too, risk shaming and loss if you come out as the parent of a child with a highly misunderstood illness. A whole lot of other people struggle privately and silently on their own, shouldering that very same weight, day in and day out.

On top of that, obtaining a mental health diagnosis can take forever (or seem to!), and the diagnosis can, and likely will, change over time. Resources, services, and treatments can be hard to find and access. There's no federal standard covering what ought to be the basics of mental health care: treatment protocols, availability and oversight of public services, the role of public education in addressing childhood mental health disorders. From state to state, you will find vastly different mental health care policies and standards; from insurance company to insurance company, you will find unequal mental/behavioral health coverage, if you find it at all.

If those are not lonely-making conditions, I don't know what would be.

Adding insult to injury is a lack of practical but *relatable* reading material out there for parents of kids with serious mental health challenges. That's why I wrote this book.

There's no twelve-step cure, no silver bullet or magic wand to make everything in your family life perfect, but it *is* possible to parent smarter, partner better, and live your own life more fully, in the shadow of childhood psychiatric illness. It's not easy, but honestly—what monumental achievement is?

What you won't find inside these pages:

- Guarantees or warranties of any kind. Because mental illness doesn't work like that.
- Lists of things to do that *will* solve all your problems (see above)
- Anything whatsoever that pretends to be one size fits all
- Explanations of what's going on inside your child's brain, where it came from, and what's coming down the road
- Names of the best clinicians, hospitals, advocates, schools, or agencies for *your* kid

What you *will* find here:

- Proof you are *not* trudging these pathways alone, even if it feels that way
- First-person stories about raising kids and teens with mental health challenges, told by real parents who've been there, done that, won some, and lost some
- Suggested strategies for supporting your struggling kid(s), your family, and yes—*you*
- Advice on dealing with ignorant or obnoxious intrusions from people close to you (and from total strangers)
- Thoughts on when and where to hide the sharp household objects
- Suggestions for locating a network of parents and supporters who get you and have your back—and blueprints for building your own networks, if you can't find the right ones ready made
- Loads of practical resources—on the web, in the community, at home, and out in the world—to help you keep doing what you do every day, only with less stress and better outcomes
- Instruction in the art and science of self-forgiveness
- Empathy, humor, and an honest reckoning of how hard your parenting job has turned out to be
- Permission to celebrate your kids just as they are, on their best days and their worst

HOW TO READ THIS BOOK

Don't look for clinical expertise or writing in these pages—I'm not a doctor or a therapist or a brain scientist. I'm a mom and an author—but even if I were the world's leading mental health expert, I *couldn't* and *wouldn't* sell you a bottle of snake oil to cure what's ailing your child. What I have to offer: thousands of hours logged parenting a kid (or two) battling serious mental health challenges and helping them pull through. I am well acquainted with trial and error, diagnostic ambiguity, heartbreaking setbacks, fear of what tomorrow will bring, and utter dread of the ultimate loss. I've sat in scores of psychiatrist offices, therapy sessions, and hospital meetings, praying silently, *Please, oh please, JUST TELL ME WHAT TO DO TO SAVE HIM AND I'LL DO IT.*

I've come to believe that the most important thing for parents like us is the offer of a compassionate hand, and a share in the wisdom of other parents and families who "get" us.

You won't find another book quite like this in the known universe of books. There are plenty of parenting manuals for people whose kids seem to be headed directly to Yale (or prom, or Wall Street, or 2.1 kids and a McMansion in suburbia) after kindergarten. There are also many smart, useful books by mental health researchers and clinicians, about your kid's specific diagnosis. And a lot of beautiful, heartrending memoirs by sufferers and survivors of agonizing mental health disorders.

Read them all, if you can! Read everything you can get your hands on. But be aware that these books may not help you in the frantic dead of night, when your kid is still manic after seventy-two hours and you're tempted to dose the two of you with brandy and Benadryl. (Don't. Seriously.) Or when you're too tired to read more than a paragraph—and if you're going to try, it's got to be one that doesn't break your heart all over again.

The book in your hands now offers you proof that you're neither hysterical nor alone; easily digestible, to-the-point advice and possible action items; and accessible resources. You can skim it in the middle of your daily panic attack, while you're on a bathroom break, or anytime you take a pause—even for just a few minutes. Its aim is to make you feel stronger and better—not overwhelmed, guilty, or more scared than you were before.

The good news is, I knew you'd have little energy or mental focus to peruse dense, technical, or lengthy books, because that's what happened to me when I got smacked by the reality of childhood mental illness.

So, just *read what you need.* Check out the table of contents, and you'll see the chapters are organized thematically, not chronologically—which means you can read this book in whatever order makes sense to you.

Each chapter focuses on one or more specific "hurdles" that most parents and kids/teens confront daily, including:

- Navigating home, school, and the outside world
- Relationships with partners, friends, and family
- Communicating with mental health providers
- Sibling issues
- Self-care and forgiveness
- And so much more

It's easy to find what chapter you need to be reading right now, because you know (or suspect) what you're struggling with, in the moment. Some "hurdles" overlap (e.g., school and relationships), and all of them will likely persist or recur, so there'll always be material for later.

Structurally speaking, every chapter in this book is similar to the others. At the start, you will always find a brief introduction, followed by a list of "Five Things I Wish I Knew from the Beginning," and at the end, "Open Mic: Kids Speak Out." In the middle, you'll find variations on some or all of the following:

- Glimpses into my own family's experiences in the trenches of childhood mental illness, along with those of other families across the country and the diagnostic spectrum
- A set of possible action items, plans, and/or suggestions for moving forward
- Useful facts, figures, and perspectives
- Links to resources (websites, blogs, support forums, books, activities, video/audio material, etc.)
- Tips on connecting with parent-allies and growing your networks
- Information-packed Q&As and FYIs from specialists: doctors, therapists, self-care experts, and others who can help you keep the ship afloat

The book contains two types of content: easily digested units, such as bulleted lists and offset text, and narrative sequences, including explanation or background and personal stories.

Varying the book's form like that was a strategic decision. For those moments when you're able to lose yourself in a story, read the longer stuff: true anecdotes from real people facing down real crises, and emerging stable enough to keep moving forward. They will remind you that resilience and peace are achievable in our own, topsy-turvy corner of the world; that success can (mysteriously) rise from the ashes of our worst screwups; and that even the slightest forward motion is something to celebrate.

Of course, sometimes, the thing you want most is to sit quietly and stare at the wall like a cat, isn't it? If you decide to pick up a book at all on days like those, the lists, strategies, and plans may be your best bet.

Just be aware that there are mighty few "sound-bite"-type utterances here. One-liners, direct assertions, and the like are for books about maladies with clear-cut diagnostic and treatment protocols. Problems that can be visualized, weighed, measured, and quantified in lab work or scans. Not here. *Our* regions of the brain are still uncharted: there be dragons here, but we don't know if they're going to kill us or just toy with us. Nor does anyone else in our orbit. What we have, at best, are hunches.

WHEN YOU'RE READING THIS BOOK
AND HEARING VOICES . . .

A brief note on the personal stories told in this book: I have removed all identifying information for the families whose stories are gathered within these pages—including names of my own husband and kids. All individuals who agreed to share their personal experiences granted me recorded or transcribed interviews, except in the rare instances where I adapted a story already told publicly in a blog post, an oral address, or another public forum (even then, I changed names if requested to, and edited for length, clarity, and style—always with permission). It felt important to me to avoid the more impersonal case study format seen in so many books about parenting unique kids. I have done my best to capture these parents' and kids' authentic voices in my re-creations of their stories, while taking care to preserve their privacy. Professionals who granted me interviews are, of course, identified and cited. Their names and affiliations as they appear in the book are their real names and affiliations.

I made certain assumptions in writing this book, based on things I've noticed in my years of connecting with other families like mine. First, the majority of parents on the mental health front line appear to be women. I believe many factors are at play here. The lingering of traditional family structures in our society, the reality that moms earn roughly $.79 on the man-dollar, and perhaps the deeply protective and proactive instincts that often seem to motivate mothers. I'm aware that this statement may not be well received by some readers—I would have scorned it too, before I had kids—but I stand by it. There are certainly exceptions. Still, my own lived experience, and that of many families in my networks, bears it out. You'll see as much from the ranks of parents and kids willing (or able) to let me interview them for the book: mostly female. I have tried my best to maintain some gender balance throughout, but it was easier to do so when writing about kids. Mental illnesses, after all, are gender blind.

Second (and this is statistically proven), marriages or partnerships often fail under the enormous strain of illness, trauma, or disability in the family. My husband Lars and I realize we've bucked the trend . . . but we are also well aware how close we've come to that edge. You may hear exasperation in some of the voices speaking within these pages. You will certainly hear it now and then in mine, when I recount some of my own family's stories of stress and survival, and my sense that this particular burden has been largely hefted on my solitary, weary back.

That doesn't mean exasperation can't coexist with love and respect. I've chosen not to shy away from any of the challenges associated with mental health parenting, but I hope I've also illustrated how, in lots of cases—certainly in my own—they are mitigated by unconditional family love, and other kinds of support.

WHY I WROTE THIS BOOK

I had some compelling reasons to create this survival guide. First, my husband and I desperately needed one like it when our family was young, but we couldn't find anything that fit the bill. And then, I knew *you* were out there: legions of stressed-out, scared, confused parents with emotionally disordered kids, trying to navigate the same wilderness I had—without a compass, or even a sun, for reference. I'm betting you're any combination of sleepless, heartsore, financially strapped, and on the brink of losing hope. I know I was.

In my many years of networking with fellow "mental health parents," I've never met one who didn't feel, at some point, like a lonely pioneer. Imagine being among the first group of adventurous (or desperate) folks to set sail for unknown continents, in search of better lives. With no survivors around to ask how things turned out when *they* disembarked on the other side, your journey would be a terrifying gamble. Well, that's a sadly relatable experience for mental health parents! Not because no one's taken this "journey" before us, but because children, their family and social environments, the particular ways any given human body may metabolize foods and medications, the accessibility of treatment options, and pretty much everything else of any relevance to our experience, *differ for everyone*. That doesn't mean we have to go it alone—it just explains why sometimes we feel so isolated.

Ultimately, maladies of the psyche are deeply personal conditions, and the brain a fickle organ. When it goes awry, in the form of a psychiatric illness, there's only so much order we can impose on the disorder. Just because *my* bipolar teen, in the grip of mania, imagines he can leap out of a moving car, somersault on the highway, and bounce to his feet unscathed like an action movie hero, doesn't mean your teen's mania will look anything like that. It *could*, but in our world, there are few consistencies. Medications, therapies, families, schools, peers, access to resources, and basic chemistry are wild cards, every one of them.

You might be wondering: If there's no standard operating manual for your kid; no key to all treatments; no reliable checklist of symptoms; no people who've lived it exactly like you have—if there's no doctor or clinic or friend or book that can tell you how to *fix everything*—then why bother with anything?

Good question! Bother because you love your kid—and because "cure" is not the only word worth knowing. Empathy, guidance, resources, and ongoing psychiatric care are only a few of many excellent, accessible healing agents. Community is another. What would I do without my comrades—the ones I know personally, and the virtual ones—in topsy-turvydom? I shudder to think! It took time to find them, but now that I have, I'm never letting go.

Folks like us are a large and growing demographic. We live in cities and towns and villages and hamlets, and we live in our own silos of anguish. We are elders and boomers and Gen-Xers and millennials. We come in every conceivable hue, shape, and socioeconomic group. We are everywhere, though our friends and neighbors may not even know it. That we are everywhere, readers, is a strange blessing. If disorders of the psyche *must* exist, then it sure helps that they exist widely.

This "mental health parenting" we undertake every day is not for the faint of heart. It can't easily be done alone. My greatest hope is that we learn to identify ourselves and each other, without judgment or shame. And then, that we find a way to come together—physically, digitally, in spirit—as a peaceful, determined army. Our mission? Get our kids, our families, and ourselves the help we need. Have each other's backs. Help change the public conversation on mental illness.

We have the potential to be a mighty force for mutual support—and even for cultural change, when we can marshal the energy and will to enter into those wider-reaching battles. Whatever you're ready for at the moment, the good news is we've found each other. Now, let's get started.

1

HOW DO YOU KNOW YOUR CHILD HAS A MENTAL HEALTH DISORDER?

Great question! It can take a lot of time, digging, and ingenuity to figure things out. Not to mention, patience and courage! Disorders of the psyche are often diagnosed only after a period of confusion and suffering that spreads through the entire household. In a young child, especially, psychiatric illness can be scary—and tough for parents to accept. Hardly a surprise, given the social stigma and misunderstanding that drive the public narrative on "mental illness." The good news is, sometimes what looks like anxiety or depression or generally off-kilter behavior in a child is a brief, passing phase, a direct response to negative external factors. But even when what appears, in your parental eyes, to be clinical depression *is* depression (or another mental illness), mental health disorders can be controlled, and stigma overcome.

KEEP CALM, AND CHECK OUT THESE STATISTICS. . . .

Typically, 1 in 5 American children have, had, or will have a seriously debilitating mental disorder by the time they reach 17.

- In 2015, that was 14 million or more kids with serious mental health issues.
- A majority of youth in American juvenile justice systems have at least one mental health condition, and at least 20 percent live with *severe* mental illness.
- Serious mental illness costs the U.S. approximately $193.2 billion in lost earnings per year.[1]

Oh, and it's never too early—or too late—to start looking for answers. So, let's get going!

FIVE THINGS I WISH I KNEW FROM THE BEGINNING

1. There is no minimum age for mental illness. If your child says or does things that seem off kilter, take it seriously—whether she's four or fourteen!
2. Your child's doctor knew what she was signing up for when she went to medical school. Don't be afraid to call her when your gut tells you to, even at inconvenient times (even three o'clock on a Sunday morning).
3. Your kid's mental health challenges are (usually) *not* your fault. Sure, they could be hereditary, but rogue genes don't ask permission before replicating themselves in our offspring.
4. Trust your parental instincts—*you know your child better than anyone.* Then fight to get him the help he deserves.
5. Take care of *you* too! Without a captain, rough seas are going to sink the ship.

OUR STORY: SNAPSHOT #1

My son Ben was four the first time he spoke about ending his life. He explained just how he'd do it: throw himself under the wheels of a truck, or out the second-story window at his preschool. He was ten the first time he begged me to help him find the best way out. At almost twelve, he asked me bluntly to kill him. Somewhere along the first third of that continuum we acknowledged something was very, very wrong with our richly loved boy. As much as you might want to, you just can't explain away a child's direct plea to assist him in his own suicide.

At some point between the preschool incident and the twelve-year-old's command that I just kill him, Ben and I held hands and listened attentively while his therapist explained where to cut his arms so he didn't end up dead. Dead was not on that day's agenda, but cutting was.

This wise therapist—who once gently informed me that yes, even when my child was only a little tyke of four, his bone-deep anxiety and depression were signs of actual "mental illness"—knew a thing or two. Benjy was going to cut whether he had our permission or not. He already had a long, complicated history of depression, anxiety, and obsessive thoughts; the crisis at hand was hardly a tiny blister on an otherwise smooth canvas. Crazy as it might sound, a kid of any age who admits he's yearning to cut his own flesh, and committed to pulling it off, is almost always telling you the truth.

So why not teach him how to do it and live? I had already learned through bitter experience that bad things can happen when a parent looks away—even for "just a moment."

That day in therapy, the adults in the room had to make a hard choice. We could take the painful step of endorsing self-harm and enabling a fourth grader to cut, releasing some of his searing inner pain, or do nothing and risk the horror of an accidental—or intentional—death. If Ben's therapist had granted me the temporary mercy of denial that day, this story might have ended years ago; dismissing *what is*, instead of dealing with it, is almost always a losing strategy. Instead he taught me to listen openly and acknowledge my son's pain. That was the day I mastered the art of distinguishing the *real* from the wished for.

When your nine-year-old has been suicidal for half his life, mere cutting looks like a relatively good deal.

Benjamin's persistent suicidal drift, his gravitation toward sharp objects and his desire to tear or slice his own skin, eventually forced my husband Lars and me to admit the unthinkable. Yes, children with fewer years of life behind them than they have fingers on one hand *could* have serious mental health challenges. No, nothing in our lives was really "normal." Maybe we would never know normal again. Maybe we'd been deceived, and normal had been a brief, convincing dream.

We may have been slow on the uptake, but when we finally grasped the truth, it was with fierce clarity: we really could lose our boy to suicide before he reached adolescence. By then, though, we were already old acquaintances with the symptoms of panic attacks, agoraphobia, paranoia, depression. We may not have had official names for every one of them, but we sure knew what they could do to a person, a family, a community.

My exhausting search for help—anything that might make our beloved son OK—started before his fourth birthday. But before I could begin searching, I had to do some mental math and accept the 2 + 2.

It was the hardest, loneliest reckoning I've ever attempted. Still, after years of fighting, losing, partial victories, and backslides, we finally reached some diagnostic and treatment breakthroughs, positive school changes, and a place of relative healing. The takeaway? Never give up hope!

WHAT'S GOING ON WITH MY KID?

Every parent wonders, off and on, what they did to deserve (or create!) the one child who can't seem to get with the program. (We're all intimately familiar with that one kid, right?) Sometimes, though, we are just making much ado about nothing. It helps to remember that every child is on their own path, and that the true beauty of people of all sorts lies in our human tendency to uniqueness.

On the other hand, sometimes we question our kids' "normalcy" out of fear. And sometimes, that fear is a perfectly appropriate response. Not all differences are created equal.

Look at it this way: while even the sunniest, most placid child or adolescent can fall apart when you least expect it, there's falling apart, and then there's *falling apart*. If you're not a trained mental health professional, or a veteran of parenting emotionally disordered kids, how are you supposed to tell the difference?

Sometimes a tantrum is just a tantrum. Mostly, cuts and bruises are expected wear and tear on growing bodies. Out-of-proportion fatigue or sleeplessness? Sadness? Apathy? Secret languages, imaginary friends and enemies? A little aggression? Hair-twisting till clumps fall out? Those are all issues that fall within the range of what we consider OK—aren't they?

Yes. But they can also be clues that something has gone wrong. We have names to describe some of these symptoms when they are severe and recurrent; the list is long.[2] Just bear in mind that psychiatric symptoms and diagnoses, especially in kids, can be maddeningly fluid, sometimes veering in unexpected directions.

So, how can you tell the difference between a little eccentricity and a brewing mental illness? Start close to home! Teachers, family, and friends can be your earliest resources; with their natural distance from you and your child, they may be better equipped than you to take in the bigger picture. You're with your kid all the time when he's little—and you may not see him that often once he hits his teens. Being too close or too distant can really mess with your perspective—which is why you'll want to enlist the help of people who can view him through a clear and (relatively) unbiased lens.

If your best friend, your mother-in-law, and Great-Uncle Gus are all suggesting there might be a problem with young Bethany, listen up. If you find yourself fielding the same comments or intercepting the same deadly glares again and again when out with your child, ask some of the people in your orbit, folks you trust, what *they* think. If they're honest, caring, and have been around the parenting block a few times, they may, by simply answering your questions, help you move forward.

"I always cave and buy Jamie something at the store—even when we're dead broke. I can't handle his constant nagging! It never ends . . . it's just this constant hunger for stuff, never satisfied! Do other kids *do* that?"

"Did your Emily pluck out her eyelashes and eyebrows when she was five years old?"

"Have you ever heard of a teenager spending days at a time shut up in his room, not eating, not talking—just being alone?"

And my favorite: "If this were your kid, would you be worried?"

If I had a nickel from every person I've asked that question, I'd be rich.

So, when should you stop thinking, *Pft, this is normal*, and start seeking professional help?

Probably just before, and right after, you've begun spending too much time Googling the stuff your child or teenager is (or isn't) doing.

The internet is a great resource for concerned parents at the beginning of their journey. But—and this is important—Google is at best your frenemy. Search the internet, by all means, but consume what you find with a generous dash of salt. When you're spending more time with Dr. Google than with your partner or your kids, you will start to realize he has no filter and brings up a lot of stuff you just shouldn't be reading. He'll blithely suggest your kid is developing Creutzfeldt-Jakob (a.k.a. mad cow) disease, or early-early-early-onset dementia—especially if you're like me, easily spooked and wildly (ahem!) "creative."

Sure, it's helpful to educate yourself before making that dreaded call to the doctor. Just proceed with caution.

USING THE INTERNET TO YOUR ADVANTAGE

Whatever your search engine, there are some easy ways to locate reliable information online when you're worried your kid might be depressed, clinically anxious, or otherwise emotionally hurting—but you're not yet ready to pick up the phone and call in a professional.

Search Smart

Search engines are not flexible thinkers. You may need to ask your questions in various ways.

Is your kid obsessed with germs? Avoiding contact with her classmates? Well, those behaviors are worth a diagnostic Google or two. Don't limit your search to "my kid is obsessed with germs," or "germaphobia," or "is my son crazy??" Instead . . .

- Ask yourself questions about the situation—your answers can provide new search terms, which may open new portals to understanding. For example: *Where and when is Jon most afraid of germs? At home? During school lunch? In public bathrooms?* All kinds of issues could be prompting your child's behaviors. Doing a bit of detective work offline can help you control what you read online.

Consider Your Source

Although we all love Wikipedia, its open-contributor policies mean its track record is somewhat spotty. Same goes for patient discussion boards (I happen to devour these almost daily, but I've learned how to read skeptically). Look for references and corroborations. Trust your gut. And check out as many alternatives as possible.

If you read "a fact" on social aggression in Wikipedia, but the Mayo Clinic and NIMH (National Institute for Mental Health) websites contradict that fact, remember: Wikipedia's open sourcing means that tidbit on social aggression might just have been penned by Great-Uncle Gus. *(You know, the old guy on your in-laws' side who hates kids—yours, in particular?)*

Be an Informed Consumer

If it looks fishy and smells fishier, you probably don't want to touch it.

You don't believe claims that those fat-free, low-carb, chocolate-encrusted-peanut-butter-marshmallow-delights with an expiration date in 2028 are good food, do you? Not really. So how come parents like us are so susceptible to shaky claims about our kids' health? Well, partly because the stakes are so high. I've gone down plenty of scary, dead-end paths myself, in desperate searches for answers—in some cases guided by dear friends who genuinely meant to help, but only convinced me my child was dying of some incurable, brain-eating disease.

Those scary dead ends are a waste of precious time and energy! Focus instead on identifying positive things you can do, while you work on obtaining reasonable and useful information. You don't have to stop (or start) with calling a professional, if it's not an emergency. Snatch whatever free moments you can—it's really OK if these are few and far between—and start learning.

Maybe you'd rather die than give your kid psych meds. Maybe you think the yoga/mindfulness/meditation side of the aisle is a joke. You might prefer to try exercise and diet to help your kid (and you) heal. It's all fine. It's all out there for you to read about, discuss, question, explore.

The bottom line? Take whatever information you encounter about child, teen, and young adult mental health as a starting point, and plan to learn as much as you can about all of it.

This is the beginning of what will likely be a long and challenging journey. Unquiet minds don't settle overnight. Kids and teens are moving targets. Therapies will work, and then they won't. You need to know that things change all the time, and use that knowledge to your advantage. Question everything, and don't stop till you find answers that make some sense in the here and now—but plan to be flexible.

Steps You Can Take Right Now (at the Beginning of Your Journey, in the Thick of It, and Anytime You Need a Reset)

- *Keep parenting!* And remember, you are the same mom or dad you were before you realized something was wrong. Your child is the same child. It's the path that's changed. Paths were *made* to accommodate detours, and—I know, it's corny—sometimes the diversion turns out to be the more scenic route.
- *Talk less, listen more.* Don't tell your kid what he's feeling and why; even the littlest and most silent sufferers will eventually open up, if you grant them the space. He may lack the descriptive language for what he's going through, but eventually you'll start to figure things out. Brainstorm with family, friends, or clinicians to crack his code. Once you do you'll be one step closer to knowing where to go from here.
- *Check in with your child's teacher and school counselor and compare notes.* These people can be valuable allies. Your home and school are the places she spends most of her time; together you may figure out which setting, if either, is more challenging for her, and why.
- *Get recommendations for good pediatric or adolescent mental health practitioners in your area.* Ask your kid's primary care doc, your family, friends, or anyone else who seems remotely clued in for names. This goes for you veteran parents as well. Sometimes, relationships with mental health professionals turn stale or sour; there's nothing wrong with shaking things up if your kid's or your needs aren't being met.
- *Make that call for advice, assistance, or just reassurance.* Better to overreact than to delay getting help.
- *Start growing a thick skin, ASAP.* Protect yourself against the rude, cruel, ignorant, and well-intentioned but offensive comments that will come your way when your kid is out of the ordinary. If you're

like me, you'll always think of the right thing to say *after* the encounter. When you do, write it down and practice saying it for the next time. Remember that other people's comments are often less about you than about their own insecurities, prejudices, and views of the way things "ought" to be. Difference can be scary—and sometimes even adults "act out" when they feel threatened. Whenever possible, keep cool, explain what you can, and walk away if you must. Practice letting people who don't understand you or your kid not matter. Life is hard enough as it is! In the end, it's *not* your job to educate, placate, or please anyone. Your job is protecting your child, your family, and you.

- *Write encouragements to yourself and post them on the bathroom mirror, or wherever you'll see them when you wake up and before you go to bed.* Currently, I have two. One says: "You are strong. You are good. You are loved and you love back. You CAN do this!" The other: "THIS IS A JUDGMENT-FREE ZONE." Honestly? They're hokey, but they help.
- *Remember, no one has this job down.* Within a few days of writing these words, I'm sure to make some high-stakes parenting fail or other. Don't be fooled: I'm better at writing about mental health parenting than I am at practicing it. As soon as you've forgiven me my failures, go forgive yourself—and take a do-over!

YOU CAN NEVER BE PREPARED: CAROLINE'S STORY

I asked Caroline, adoptive mom to seventeen-year-old Will, how she came to terms with his inner turmoil, and what parenting him over the years has looked and felt like.

Caroline: I became a foster mom to a little boy named Will on December 4, 2003. He was not even five when I first met him on the inpatient pediatric psychiatry floor at a local hospital. I was in grad school at the time, and when I met him he just stole my heart. He was so adorable—a little boy with a bright smile and a fun personality. He was that kid who totally lit up the room.

Unlike most parents whose children turn out to have mental illnesses, I did know, in some sense, what I was getting into from the get-go. His social worker told me the first three and a half years of Will's life were a nightmare. He was physically and sexually abused and neglected. It would truly break your heart to hear this stuff. She also warned me about some of his troubling behaviors, which, of course, are to be expected in a kid with such a traumatic start.

I started imagining Will as my own son—new life, new home, a mom who would love him and protect him. I should have known better, but I was convinced that with stability and lots of love, he would be totally fine, not to worry. You know, what parent doesn't believe in the healing power of their love?

Thank goodness I believed in my love! Because, when Will became available for adoption, I didn't hesitate for a minute to become his forever mom.

Oh, boy. Even with my master's degree in mental health counseling, and knowing his history, I wasn't really prepared for the chaos he would bring into my home. You never can be prepared for something like that, anyway. He was different than he had been in the hospital. He hoarded animal crackers because he was afraid there would be no more the next day. Trashed his bedroom at night, because he was scared for his safety while he slept. Urinated on the floor out of anger. He couldn't get close to me, or let me get close to him—not for a long time, at least.

Sometimes I'd wake up to the smell of the feces he'd hidden in the radiators of his room. The poor baby was scared to go to the toilet in the middle of the night. He was scared of the bath, he screamed and kicked when I ran a bubble bath for him. I later learned he associated the bath with being sexually molested and burned. The sadness in that is . . . it's just, beyond anything you've ever felt.

When Will's been in the grip of his illnesses (bipolar disorder, autism, PTSD, and RAD—reactive attachment disorder) he has beaten me and my wife Jennifer up. Destroyed our things. Hurt himself, collapsed in rage and sadness, been aggressively oppositional. He has half scared us to death—on our behalf and his.

So, yeah—raising Will is the hardest thing I've ever done, but it's also the best! Twelve years later, I wouldn't change things for the world.

I'm sure I'll be figuring out how to best parent Will forever. I'm OK with that. I was committed to making him a good life, and that continues to be my priority—and a work in progress. The great news is, with the help of an excellent residential school, he's thriving! All that's precious in Will—his sweet nature, his goodness, his intelligence, his drive to do well and do good—has been growing and blossoming. Love by itself is probably not enough to heal a child like Will. But love, plus the right educational and therapeutic setting and supports, seems to be doing the trick. If I know for sure just one thing in life, it's that I will never give up on my son, or stop loving him. I'm so grateful we found each other!

WHAT DO MOST PEOPLE KNOW ABOUT CHILDHOOD MENTAL HEALTH DISORDERS?

Try this: ask your friends to guess the third-leading cause of death among kids. (Yep, it's suicide.) This heartbreaking statistic can give you the opportunity to start a conversation about childhood mental health disorders. The more we talk about this, the better for everyone.

SOMETHING'S WRONG WITH MY KIDS? I THINK THEY'RE JUST RIGHT: DIERDRE'S STORY

Dierdre and her husband have two young adult daughters, both of whom have lived with various emotional disorders since childhood. I asked what tipped her off to the fact that something was amiss, how she dealt with that knowledge at the start, and how she's handling things now.

Dierdre: It took me a while to put two and two together and recognize my two daughters' anxiety and depression for the mental illnesses they are. And that's kind of odd, because anxiety, depression, and bipolar disorder run in my immediate family. To me, the girls—who are two years apart and very alike in many ways—always seemed to function exactly as they were supposed to when they were younger. A lot like I did at their ages, in fact. So, you know, Dierdre-normal. Six-hour crying jags? Yep, I did that. Hypersensitivity at school and in social situations? Always the ones unsettled by classroom conflict—to the point of not managing to stay put in the classroom? It was all familiar to me, and at first, we just lived it without overthinking it. The thing is, I'd never thought of myself as someone with "mental health issues"—so I didn't look at my daughters through that prism.

Of course, I couldn't deny forever that there were problems. As they grow older, I think kids become psychologically more complicated—as does their world. So, the severe mood swings, hours of tears, and extreme sensitivity in social situations became more and more disabling for my teenage daughters. There was some cutting, some eating and body-image issues, and a few psychiatric hospitalizations, as well as physical health conditions that I believe are related to their emotional dysregulation. Every day was (and is) a challenge.

I still don't like labels. I still see my daughters as just right the way they are. So, here's a question I ask myself all the time: Why are the supersensitive kids like mine—the anxious, shy, emotional ones—perceived as "disordered"? Our culture views people who generate conflict, who bully, who feel confidence in themselves but not much empathy for others, as charismatic. As "winners." Maybe that's the problem? Just something worth considering.

RESOURCES: PEOPLE, PLACES, BOOKS, WEBSITES, AND APPS

First things first: your most valuable resource in this whole wide world (apart from the people in your life who love you and yours, unconditionally) will turn out to be the Rest of Us. We're everywhere, we "get" you, and we *want* to help you—just like others help, have helped, and continue to help us. Seriously, don't try taking this trip solo.

You can find us in the flesh and in online groups. At the end of a phone line. Standing around outside your kid's school (often connecting with other "disability parents"). Reach out to us! If you don't know who we are, email the leader of your school district's Special Education Parent Advisory Council and ask for an introduction to other families like yours. You can even request that a school guidance counselor, a teacher, or your kid's therapist help you connect. Privacy laws prohibit them providing you a list of names, but you can always offer your name and contact information, and request they be forwarded to some appropriate parents. I promise, you'll hear from someone.

And if you search online, you'll find lots of websites, blogs, and social media groups created just for parents like you, devoted to mutual education and support. Join them and start talking! Tell your story, ask questions, and offer advice. These are the people who, each in their own ways, small or great, will help you survive and thrive. (See chapter 2 for more details on in-person and online support.)

Pros: You can cry on our shoulders and smear your wet mascara all over our shirts. We've been there, and done that.

Cons: Our topics of discussion can be a downer, and sometimes we traffic in dark humor. Hey, it's a coping mechanism.

Other Places to Learn and Connect

ONLINE

National Alliance on Mental Illness (www.NAMI.org)
NAMI is a lifeline for many Americans facing the devastation of dealing with psychiatric disorder. It exists as a national organization with

regional chapters. I learned about NAMI through the friend of a friend as I was groping in the dark and beginning to grow my network. Go here to access all kinds of resources, including a toll-free helpline, blogs and articles, videos, and discussion groups aimed at fostering mental health education, advocacy, and community. NAMI also offers free, in-person education/support programs for parents and caregivers in certain regions.

Pros: Great source of information and support, and an organization that "gets it."

Cons: Somewhat more useful in theory than in practice—to me, at least. In-person programs can be far flung, so if you live outside metropolitan areas (or somewhere NAMI has no active volunteers) you might be out of luck. I found it difficult to figure out how to join the online discussion group for parents of kids with mental illness; could have been depleted-brain syndrome on my part, or a usability flaw on the site. And finally, if you look deeply into the discussion forums you will need a box of tissues—there are some impossibly sad stories in the microcosm you and I inhabit.

www.Psychcentral.com

In the vein of psychologytoday.com but more practically focused, this site caters to the layperson who wants access to mental health information, resources, or just a bit of psychoeducation. (If you are a parent *and* a "mental health pro," just click on over to the clinical edition!) Helpful blogs, articles, clinical trial alerts, online discussion boards, and more can be found here. What I especially like about this site is that it categorizes by diagnosis, so if your kid has schizophrenia you can easily bypass content about unrelated stuff if you want to.

Cons: I'm waiting (im)patiently for the app!

BOOKS

My Feeling Better Workbook: Help for Kids Who Are Sad and Depressed by Sara Hamil, LCSW (2008)

I'm Not Bad, Just Mad: A Workbook to Help Kids Control Their Anger by Anna Greenwald, Zack Pelta-Heller, and Lawrence Shapiro, PhD (2008)

The Relaxation and Stress Reduction Workbook for Kids: Help for Children to Cope with Stress, Anxiety, and Transitions by Lawrence Shapiro, PhD, and Robin Sprague (2009)

These "help for kids" books are just a few samples from a workbook series. As their titles suggest, they share a common denominator (mental health) but branch out in specific directions. (There are workbooks specifically written for teens too.) If you can get your struggling child to actually sit down and take a look—more easily done when she or he is not in crisis—you may see a positive response. At the very least, these workbooks have the power to show children with mental health disorders that they are not alone—and definitely not a lost cause. I like these because they show kids how to take steps to help themselves. By doing so, they instill in their young readers a sense of empowerment and responsibility.

Pros: They pack a punch in a short and easy-to-use format.

Cons: Good luck convincing your already stressed-out youngster this isn't homework but something better. (Full disclosure: I am a veteran loser of this battle.)

EXPRESSLY FOR YOU, READER!

You know how you never paid attention when the flight attendant told you to "put the oxygen mask on yourself first, then on your children"? It turns out the flight attendant was on to something.

Your kid needs you to take care of yourself.

On the off chance you'll consider this advice and look after yourself, I've listed some resources specifically for you. On the very good chance you will not, because simply taking a shower can be a fearsome feat of juggling these days, that's OK. Tomorrow you can try again!

Mindfulness, Meditation, and Yoga

There's a reason meditation and yoga have become cool, and it doesn't involve designer body-wear.

They work!

If you are like me, your mind is always racing from the recent past, to the here and now, to way out there in the "probable" future, and back again. Meditation (or mindfulness) can help slow it down. When your mind is still, your body can relax. When your mind is quiet and your body is relaxed, life gets better—even when life is flinging boulders at your head.

I'm not saying doing these good-for-you things is easy. I suppose it could be, but parents like us have precious little time to devote to breathing and bodily contortion. We're tired. Cynical. Bummed out. And too busy keeping our families afloat to bother with this relaxation stuff.

But—even five minutes of mindful breathing or gentle yoga a day can help. And once you carve out those five minutes, it may seem worthwhile to carve out five more.

When you're ready to try, all you really need is some guidance and a quiet space. A simple internet search will yield a lot of websites that can teach you to focus on breathing, balance, and bodily and emotional wellness.

I like the following online and mobile resources, but there are many more, lots of them free, that can help you reconnect with yourself. And they may work magic for your kids too, if you feel inclined to try.

ONLINE

www.mindful.org

I love this site, and bookmarked it as soon as I stumbled upon it (way too many years into this journey). It offers all kinds of resources and information to help you de-stress. Excellent guided meditations, easy-to-digest articles on living and working mindfully, and more. Whenever I have a ten-minute break, I try to head here.

Pros: Well organized, nonintimidating, both theoretical and practical.

Cons: Not easily used on the go; featured meditations may require significant time commitment.

www.doyogawithme.com

Free yoga videos for most levels and needs. I like this online mode because I can stop when I'm spent, or modify poses, and no old ladies are going to humiliate me by leaving me in the dust. Yoga in general is good for your bodily and mental health. If you can get the whole family involved, all the better.

Pros: It's free! Plus, you can do this yoga in torn pajamas, with unbrushed hair and teeth, and it just won't matter. If you're uncoordinated like me, no one will ever know that, either.

Cons: You're on your own, baby. No community of yogis except the improbably attractive and supple folks in the videos. Also, for me, yoga has always felt intimidating. I have chronic pain. I'm stiff. The poses scare me. So, in my case, this yoga business is a work in progress. For you, it might be just what the doctor ordered.

MOBILE

Mindfulness

Free and/or inexpensive guided meditations, right on your smartphone. Choose the voice (male, female), the type, the duration in minutes. You can also easily program in canned text notifications (*Bing!* "Would you like to meditate?"). Or script your own. ("Relax your shoulders." "Breathe in and out." "Notice your surroundings." And my favorite: "Put down the damn phone!")

Pros: Portable, light on the wallet, easy to use. Good for folks with limited time and resources.

Cons: Easy to ignore the notifications you so carefully arranged to go off at random intervals, and just keep fighting-or-flighting through your day instead.

Virtual Hope Box

A friend and fellow mental health parent introduced this to me when I was wildly stressed and running in several directions at once but getting nowhere. I love it!

Designed for veterans with PTSD, this is a great app for people trying to heal from any kind of trauma. If you're reading this book, you are likely one of those people. It offers several paths to inner calm: "Distract Me" (puzzles, word searches, etc.); "Inspire Me" (thoughtful, empowering quotes from famous and anonymous people); "Relax Me" (guided meditations, other coping tools); "Activity Planner" (this one speaks for itself); and "Remind Me" (a place to upload and access your own favorite music, photos, video clips, etc.).

Pros: Free and portable. A beautiful, thoughtfully designed app. Makes me feel grateful someone remembered that a lot of folks out there are dealing with trauma. Great collection of de-stressors and self-care activities.

Cons: At first glance, seems like it's going to be too much work. Took me awhile to muster the energy to take a second look. But you don't have to put much effort into it, if you don't care to personalize it.

Calm.com

This one's a keeper. Not so different than other mindfulness apps, but I love the option to listen to a "sleep story" (they work, I promise!), nature sounds, and a bunch of different meditations. And it curates offerings based on your goals (for example, stress or anxiety management, focus, sleep, gratitude, self-esteem, and more).

Pros: It's flexible and offers a substantial amount of quality content. (Why, hello there, *Sleep Stories!* And *Calm Masterclass!*) Plus, the nature sounds are realistic—and the birdsong will probably not drive you crazy if you're anything like me and hyperparticular about which birds are included.

CLINICAL FYI: THIS THERAPY CAN HELP YOU HEAL

You know that expression, "You're only as happy as your least happy child"? I'll bet whoever coined it was one of us! We know too well how parents, fighting to save a child in the grip of mental illness, can succumb to their own fear and sadness.

I asked Boston-area therapist Jessica Reed, LICSW (certified IFS therapist), to suggest a way parents like us can take care of ourselves. Jessica recommends internal family systems (IFS) therapy. (I've tried it. It's powerful, and worth considering.)

DV: What is IFS therapy?
JR: IFS is different from some better-known therapies, like CBT (cognitive behavioral therapy). IFS views personality and psychotherapy through the lens of an internal "family"—people being made up of a core Self, and a series of Parts, all of which continually interact with each other. Every person is endowed with a core Self, but that Self can be buried under a lot of protective Parts—aspects of our internal selves that develop over the years, and whose sole objective is to protect our vulnerable young and exiled parts from seeing the light of day. Unfortunately, the end result is that these "protected" parts often cause more pain, not less. Only when we learn to identify and love *all* our Parts (the whole internal "family"), can we access our core Selves and find wholeness.

DV: How does it help?
JR: An IFS therapist teaches clients to see all their Parts, no matter how extreme, as emerging to help them cope with painful feelings. The saying "All Parts are welcome" is essential to IFS therapy. Rather than banishing or replacing the feelings/behaviors that give us emotional trouble, IFS fosters healing by helping clients develop a loving relationship between Self and Parts. A deep and long-lasting healing occurs when we are empowered to love all aspects of ourselves, rather than seeing some of them simply as destructive behaviors.

In other words, it works by aiding us in getting in touch with all the parts of our inner Selves, and in practicing self-compassion.

IFS therapy is especially suited to people dealing with issues like trauma, fragile self-esteem, and severe anxiety—people who have trouble valuing or accepting themselves. It is ultimately forgiving of setbacks and relapses. Not only does IFS therapy help my clients heal, but I find that I am helped by it too, personally and professionally.

DV: Where can readers learn more, and how can they find an IFS practitioner?

JR: Readers can learn more about IFS at the Center for Self Leadership (www.selfleadership.org), where they will find information about the model and a list of IFS therapists located around the country.[3]

TAKING CARE OF ME: OUR STORY, SNAPSHOT #2

Almost five years ago, after enduring ten years of relentless high stress, sleeplessness, and what I later learned to call emotional trauma, I sat down with an old family friend and held out my hand.

Dr. Leon Hammer had trained as a psychiatrist, but long ago turned to healing patients through acupuncture and herbal medicine. He was my father's oldest friend. He'd known me a long time. He knew my son was anxious, severely depressed, and prone to self-harm. And really, he had only to look at me to see that I was also growing sick.

This was the second time, in my thirteen years of being a mother, that Dr. Hammer had read my pulses. For the second time in thirteen years he found my "Qi," or life force, to be dangerously feeble.

I was so tired. I kept nodding off while his fingers sought the faint flutter in my wrists. Everything hurt. I updated him, in between thirty-second naps, on life at home with Lars, Saskia, and Benjy. I used words like "knives," and "self-harm," and "psych ward" way more often than any parent of a couple of preteen kids should have to. (Zero times would seem about right.)

He pressed my two hands between his, once he'd learned what he needed to know from the ebb and flow of my blood.

"Debbie," he said, gazing straight at me, "I need to tell you a story. I was a navigator in the Second World War. We flew in a bomber over Germany. Every time our squadron went out on a mission, we knew that fifty percent of us would not be coming back. We didn't talk about it—we just knew it. But I would take that over what you've been living, hands down."

Talk about crazy! Those words woke me up fast. I tried to protest with what energy I had.

"This is nothing," I rasped, "compared to what a soldier does. How could it be? I'm not going to die! Not now, anyway."

He just looked at me with his steady, quiet eyes. He wasn't going to back down.

Maybe it was the lack of boundaries in Ben's mental illness—his uncontainable and completely unpredictable mood swings and behaviors— that made Dr. Hammer feel the way he did about my situation. At least you can wrap your head around fifty-fifty odds. You can learn by feel the interior of a B–24 bomber if you must, and you can memorize a slew of flight paths across Europe. I'm sure World War II felt endless to the many who suffered through it. All wars must feel that way. But if you were a young American navigator like Leon, who knew the rules of engagement, and also knew that no war in history had lasted forever, perhaps you could occasionally see peace on the horizon.

I couldn't even see the horizon, let alone peace. There were barely any days—even hours or minutes in a row—I could let my guard down. If I did, I might stumble into a parent's worst nightmare and never get out. If I turned away a few minutes too long, I might lose the son I so dearly loved.

Leon Hammer knew this. My face, my gait, my feeble pulse told all. He loved me and wanted to send me a message. This stuff is as hard as it gets—and I had his permission to believe it and acknowledge it, without apology or shame. I had his permission to see myself as a soldier—capable of a soldier's immense courage and susceptible to a soldier's mental anguish. Once I saw my own suffering as serious and real, I could justify offering myself the care I needed. Reader, I am passing that permission on to you.

OPEN MIC: KIDS SPEAK OUT!

Robby, Age Seventeen, New Hampshire

I didn't necessarily think something was wrong with me at first. I only knew that school was hell, from kindergarten on. I would always be confused in class, so I would lay my head down and try to sleep. Sometimes I slept in the nurse's office all day. It was all scary. Cafeteria: scary. Bathrooms: scary. Playground. You never knew what kids were gonna do. There were a lot of bullies who hated kids like me. Sometimes teachers were insensitive. They'd out me when they caught me secretly biting off my fingertips at my desk, they'd be like, "Robby, what's wrong with your hands, what's that, blood?" And everyone would look at me like I was some type of weird bug, which made me need to bite my fingers even more. The finger biting was in fourth or fifth grade. And I believed them, I was just this weird bug in the wrong habitat.

I wanted to die starting, I don't know, before elementary school, basically. My life was always like one giant cringe. I guess I realized something was wrong with that—like, you know, not every kid felt like that, secretly, in their heart—when my mom started taking me all over the state to doctors and therapists, and everyone acted concerned about me. I was maybe in third grade when I realized I wasn't what people call "normal."

It's a lot better now. I have some names for what I've got (one of them is "mood disorder"), and I've met other kids like myself, in the hospital and at my school. Stuff can still be hard, but I feel stronger and more successful than when I was a little kid.

THE TAKEAWAY

In General

- Assume it's serious.
- Educate yourself as best you can.
- Get professional advice and treatment when needed.
- Find "The Rest of Us" and tap into our support networks.
- Take care of *you*.

When It's Not an Emergency
(i.e., Everyone Is Safe/No One Is Incapacitated)

- Put the internet to good use.
- Ask friends, family, and teachers about behaviors they've seen.
- Don't believe everything you read or hear.
- Consult your child's pediatrician.
- Learn to evaluate advice from experts and amateurs alike; tune out the unhelpful, and explore the reasonable.
- Be open to everything, and skeptical about everything.
- Don't give up in the face of detours and roadblocks!

When Things Feel Unsafe

Get up from your diagnostic Googling and seek professional help, especially if:

- Your child's actions seem off kilter and inexplicable, and you're pretty sure it's not the result of too many jelly beans and licorice sticks in one sitting.
- Her personality changes markedly—increased aggression, isolation, sadness, or anxiety, for example—and for longer than you think is reasonable, given the circumstances. Every child is unique; you know yours better than anyone else.
- He loses skills or knowledge of any kind, which could point to a serious medical and/or psychiatric issue.
- You're scared, and/or he's scared, for his or anyone else's safety.

In an Emergency

- Tap family or friends who can help take care of other children if you're called away. (It's best to have a plan set up in advance, so you don't waste time figuring out whom to call, and other logistics.)
- Know how to get to the nearest emergency room or crisis center. Know the best route and how long it will take you to get there by car. If you can (and there's more than one option), find out *before* you need to use it which ER has a pediatric/adolescent section and whether one or more nearby hospitals offers inpatient psychiatric treatment.
- Figure out in advance whether 911 is a call you're prepared to make, and understand what may happen if you do.

Most of all: show your child your love is unconditional—even when that feels hard to do.

U.S. CRISIS HOTLINES

For a longer list, see https://psychcentral.com/lib/telephone-hotlines-and-help-lines/.

- Crisis Help Line—For Any Kind of Crisis   800-233-4357
- Parental Stress Hotline—Help for Parents   800-632-8188
- U.S. Suicide Hotline   800-784-2433
- NDMDA Depression Hotline—Support Group   800-826-3632
- Suicide Prevention Services Crisis Hotline   800-784-2433

2

AT HOME WITH MENTAL ILLNESS / MENTAL ILLNESS AT HOME

No one's ever quite "at home" with the experience of psychiatric disorder. Not in the sense of feeling at ease, nurtured, and protected.

So, what's with the chapter title?

You can take it literally—as in, you live in a place you call "home," and you do your best to manage the challenges of a child's mental illness within that home. (Mental illness at home.) Or, you can take it as a sense of how we experience life: if we know and accept ourselves and our loved ones as we *are*—people who live in the eye of an emotional hurricane—we may begin to feel more "at home" in our minds, in our bodies, and with our own particular "normal." (At home with mental illness.)

It all makes perfect sense, but that doesn't mean it's easy.

Still, you *can* find ways to live with the challenges of mental illness at home, and learn to *feel* at home with them too. Let's get started.

FIVE THINGS I WISH I KNEW FROM THE BEGINNING

1. For families like ours, sometimes home is a safe place—but sometimes it's not.
2. Everyday household items can become weapons. Not just knives and scissors: shoelaces, pencils, medications. Know where they are, when and how to hide them.
3. You and your kid probably won't make it out of the house as often as you think you should. This is your normal; don't beat yourself up over it.
4. When things go really wrong, you may feel tempted to lash out at your kid and others, self-destruct, or just give up. *Please*, don't!

Life gets better—even if only now and then. When it does, regroup, replenish, and recommit to the good fight.

5. Enjoy those quiet moments. If you spend all your time worrying about the next shoe dropping, you'll miss the good stuff.

OUR STORY: SNAPSHOT #3

Once our babies grew up enough to resist eating paint chips and plugging little fingers into electrical outlets, Lars and I decided it was OK to ditch the babyproofing devices. We figured if both kids proved they understood the logic behind certain household rules—for example, kids still using blunted scissors at school don't get to use the sharp knives, the oven, or grandma's sewing kit at home—they were basically safe in the house.

That was when I still believed in the power of logical thinking to keep things in order. Of course, I knew early on that Benjy's mental health was unreliable; that he was a card-carrying depressive and anxious person; that he'd talked, on and off, about wanting to end his life. But I also believed he was physically safe at home because he was always at home with an adult—and because we didn't have guns in our house. So, when he'd ask to go down to the basement "kid cave" for some solo time on the Wii, I'd say yes—even if he seemed a little off kilter. Especially when I was stuck with a pile of freshman English papers to grade, and needed some space of my own.

It's still hard to avoid blaming myself for poor judgment. He was nine years old. Enjoying a little Super Mario in the cave? Why not—everyone else's kids were!

Except, most of them weren't also harboring a desire to hurt themselves.

I'd be grading essays and wondering if a bottle of wine would raise everyone's grade a notch or two, when up from the basement would float a strangulated scream.

"Ben!" I'd scream back, shedding leaves of student work everywhere in my mad rush toward the basement stairs. "Are you okay?"

"I'm fine, Ma," he'd say, sounding fine, his voice measured and firm.

"Why did you scream, then?"

"I was just frustrated. Don't worry about it, I'm good."

"Okay," I'd say, retreating to my makeshift desk at the dining room table. I *had* to believe him, because there were twenty essays left to grade, and God knows we needed the small change I earned as an adjunct professor. Eventually I gave myself permission not to react. He said he was fine, he sounded fine. No problem.

These were not among my bravest moments, but I'd like to believe I have always done the best I could at any given time. Obviously, my best can be severely mediocre. It took some suspicious marks on his body, the kind you can't reason away, to finally wake me up.

One evening, Ben felt the weight of the universe pressing on his heart, and he asked for a calming bath. Warm baths were one of his coping devices. An occasional glass of wine was one of mine. Though he was in fourth grade, he had absolutely no modesty; he liked me to sit on the closed toilet with my half glass of Riesling and keep him company.

I listened patiently to his chatter (it would be several years before we understood these hypermonologues as explicit signs of mania). At some point, my eyes flicked over him and I noticed the usual bruises on his legs. Like always, I reminded myself: *Nine-year-old boys have bruises. This is normal.* But this time I looked closer, and saw one large bruise on each of his thighs, in the exact same place on each leg. I licked the rim of my wineglass and reflected on the perfect symmetry of those dark spheres.

It took longer than it should have to register as . . . very wrong.

"What are those?" I pointed to his legs.

He glanced offhand at his thighs. "Bruises?"

"How did they get there? So evenly placed."

He shook his head. Finally, in a tiny voice, he said, "Hit myself." He scrutinized my face, trying to read me. I looked down. There was a fruit fly drowning in my Riesling.

"I want out, Mom." He stood up, and little streams of bathwater rushed down his belly and over his battered legs.

It turned out Benjy had been hitting himself for months. There were other indications of self-harm that we'd failed to recognize. His mutilated fingertips, his bitten and shredded inner cheeks, his lower lip, chewed purple black, weren't just the "compulsions" that can go along with OCD or Tourette's disorder, though that's what we thought we saw. I myself am a lifelong cuticle picker, my thumbnails forever ridged like a turtle's back. What Benjy did never seemed that different from my own picking.

It was.

Only when I saw those perfect bruises, and shortly thereafter caught him with a pair of pointed scissors, trying to work up the nerve to cut himself, did the message finally sink in: a period of upbeat chattiness now and then was no guarantee of good mental health. Even worse, *home was not a guaranteed safe zone for our family.*

That felt like waking from a nightmare, only to realize the nightmare was real life.

MENTAL ILLNESS AT HOME

Time at home can be hard for mental health families, especially those with few, if any, supports in place. Just managing everyday stuff—downtime in the apartment or house, chores, recreation, errands, appointments, meals, sibling relationships, and so on—poses a real challenge when one or more family members is emotionally disordered.

You know the deal. After school, your six-year-old is humming the soundtrack from *Frozen* and coloring with his favorite scented markers; by dinnertime he's sobbing, knocking his head on the table, kicking the dog, and fighting to draw enough breath to tell you he is not worthy of living. You've got to figure out what's the best response, how long is this likely to last, is everyone safe? Who's going to tend to what and whom, until the microburst passes? Of course, the microburst could grow into a relentless, raging hurricane, in which case the passing could take days or weeks.

There may be siblings caught in the middle of the storm. Pets, friends. You may be the only adult on the scene. You'll need to make some tricky decisions. Do you give him his PRN ("as needed") anxiety pill? Maybe a Benadryl? Do you medicate him with a video, or a double cheeseburger and fries? Promise to buy him the hamster he's been bugging you about for the past six weeks? And what are you supposed to do about any other kids in the house?

All excellent questions! Unfortunately, I can't offer you a personalized, guaranteed, bona fide crisis-buster program. (I wish I could, though!) Nor can your child's mental health provider, although he or she may help you feel your way through the dark.

Here's why: our kids aren't machines. Moods change by the hour, even the minute. So do behaviors. What helps today may hurt tomorrow. Children and adolescents are inconsistent even at the peak of health and "normal." When they're emotionally disordered, the most solid parenting wisdom in the universe just doesn't apply. For parents like us, there are no universally proven practices, no general operating instructions, no reasons whatsoever to expect the expected.

In our corner of the world, sometimes two plus two is just going to be eleven, no matter how strongly we fight that strange calculus.

Not every "midnight meltdown" warrants paging the psychiatrist or a call to the crisis team. Sometimes, that dreaded phone message from the school counselor simply means you've gotta pick up your kid, who needs a safe space to chill out and regroup, and take her home. At other times, you may be facing an escalation that requires professional intervention. Things can resolve or get worse in a flash. All you can really do is be watchful and nimble—in other words, *be mentally prepared*. Eventually, you'll get pretty good at making the right call.

Fortress or Minefield?

Sometimes home life is a breeze—everyone's happy, busy, or sleeping peacefully. Other times, not so much. There may be dragons in your basement and daggers in your cupboards, but you *live* in that home—and so does your family. You can't avoid it. Which is fine, because notwithstanding its perils, you'll sometimes find hunkering down in the house to be the best of a few lousy options. At least you maintain a modicum of control over the environment there, versus out in public.

It'll take some effort, but you *can* find ways to make your home a relatively safe place for you and your family—despite the mental illness(es) that reside there with you.

You've Got to Have a Home Plan

As soon as you're ready, start mapping out a "home plan." You won't need one on a daily basis, but when you do need it, you'll be glad you have it. Your home plan doesn't have to be complicated.

Even if you're more of a seat-of-the-pantser than a mapper and planner, it's crucial to have strategies up your sleeve for addressing psychiatric escalation at home. If it makes you feel any better, I fall clearly into the pantser camp—chronically dreamy, disorganized, easily stressed. I know myself well enough to admit I'm not going to develop executive-functioning superpowers at this late stage. And that's OK; even without fully developed organizational skills, I've learned through trial and error (lots and lots of error) what to do—and not to do—when crisis strikes at home. Yep—I've got a home plan etched in my brain. And so, reader, can you.

Keep reading to see why *all* mental health parents need one.

SCENARIO 1

You've been called at work by one of the school counselors. "You need to pick your son up immediately, because he's sure not welcome in chemistry lab with *that* explosive behavior." By "explosive behavior," the counselor means scary, verbal aggression.

Let's say your son (we'll call him Jake) suffers from schizoaffective disorder, and lately his symptoms have been aggravated. Adding insult to injury, the counselor who calls is the judgmental one you secretly hate. Someone is going to have to leave work immediately, get Jake safely home, and keep the world from tilting off its axis.

SCENARIO 2

You've got a thirteen-year-old daughter with major depression and a debilitating anxiety disorder. It doesn't help that she's overweight and cognitively blunted from her psych meds. Ostracized and bullied by classmates (and even certain staff at her middle school), she grabs a paper clip from her teacher's supply shelf and walks out of French class, unnoticed. Alone in the restroom she locks herself in a stall, unfurls the clip, pushes up her sleeve, and carves three letters into the underside of her forearm: D.I.E. Then she slides down her sleeve and goes back to her classroom.

No one observes the blood sopping into her shirt, but you see the stains the moment she gets off the bus and enters the house—and so does her toddler brother, who runs up, pats her tender arm, and shrieks, "Boo-boo!"

THE FALLOUT

OK, so you're home with your child, and your child is not in good shape. To complicate matters, life is . . . well, complicated. You have other commitments, others who rely on you, and certainly not least important, your personal needs. An eye-opening moment in my own life was the day an attending psychiatrist at a Boston inpatient psych unit gifted me the following ten words, each humble on its own but fiercer together: "Childhood mental illness does not take place in a vacuum." Families, friends, finances,

It goes without saying that not every crisis is a *crisis*. Sometimes, a quiet reboot at home fixes everything. Other times, things go downhill, fast. Problem is, you can't always predict which way it's headed. What can you do while you're caught in limbo, between resolution and escalation, and need to stay safely put at home? Activate your home plan!

bodily wellness, even entire communities must absorb its blows, along with your child and you. Still, with some practice and a plan, you can manage your child's illness outside the vacuum. Not always well, but perfection is one of the first myths busted in disability circles anyway.

A Home Plan Looks Like This

Your home plan won't likely be a formal, typed-out document. On the contrary: after weathering a few—or a few hundred—of these events, you'll sense what works with your kid and what doesn't, and what to do in the moment. I like to refer to what we parents do as "informed improvisation." Learn the basic "rules of engagement," and go from there—knowing you'll make mistakes along the way.

1. Play it safe.
   - Hide the cooking knives, scissors, razors, and even his shoelaces. (They take all strings and laces away before allowing kids on the hospital psych unit. I'm sure you can imagine why.) You'll never get them all, because you can't foresee everything that can be weaponized. Decent hidey holes include Dad's underwear drawer, the bottom of a basket of dirty laundry, or any other place your kid is guaranteed not to look or be able to access.
   - Ditto for household medications: prescription and over-the-counter drugs, vitamins and supplements, mouthwashes, antiseptic washes, and so on. Lock them up or hide them where your kid will never think to look.
   - Cleaning supplies can be deadly. If you feel you need to hide those too, do it. Consider responsibly dumping the toxic stuff and using natural, DIY products instead. Vinegar, baking soda, and lemon can work wonders, and recipes for making your own stash of cleaning products are all over the internet. As far as I know, no one was ever poisoned with baking soda or lemons.
   - Got alcohol in the house? Use your judgment: if your psychiatrically involved child is in primary school, you're probably safe keeping it on hand. Got a teen with addictive or impulsive tendencies (or just a teen in general)? Give it away, lock it up, or ask a friend to hang on to it for you. Or just go out for drinks—presuming there comes an evening when all your stars align.
   - Make sure you know how to access a bedroom or bathroom with doors that lock from the inside. Seriously. Better yet, replace the

hardware. I know, it sucks. It can be a day's work (or too much money, if you've got to hire someone else to do it for you), but it's worth it. On the other hand, you could always learn how to pick locks fast, while keeping your cool.

- If there are firearms in your house, *keep them unloaded and locked away, at all times.* This is mental health parenting 101—don't fail it.

2. Supervise.

- Watch him like an owl—that is, keenly but stealthily. (Kids and teens don't always seem to appreciate parental surveillance—no surprise there!—but when their agitation is escalating, your hovering presence could make things worse.)
- Take note of her body language. You'll learn to assess your child's psychiatric status by watching her face, her eyes, her posture, her hands, her movements, and so on.
- Find an excuse to eyeball him every twenty minutes, or however often feels right to you. You *do* need to get in there to collect that moldering laundry, you know, or to offer him some of those brownies you just remembered you baked (or bought) and froze last week. Or to get him talking about whatever floats his boat.
- Listen for clues to his condition in his speech or tone of voice. Some red flags: unusually low or high pitch; pressured, rapid speech; confused, garbled, or threatening talk; unexpected silence, or anything significantly out of character.
- If necessary, simply stand outside her closed bedroom door and listen. Knock, ask her questions, barge in if you feel you must. (Crisis time is *not* the time to start thinking about locks on doors and what to do about them.)

3. Connect.

- Let her know you've got her back. Remind her that you're here to listen, that your love is unconditional, and that you will never judge her for the things her illness does.
- Ask his permission for (appropriate) physical contact—a hug, a back rub, sitting close, side by side on the couch. There is much to be said for the healing power of touch, barring sensory aversions to it. If he declines, let him know that's totally fine—and try not to let him see any hurt or dismay you might be feeling.
- Use distraction to help him get outside his own head, where he may be drowning in his own distorted thoughts. Show him

funny cat videos, or ask for a tutorial on memes (the latter tack may work best on younger kids; I asked my teens for feedback on the idea, and they just laughed at me and said, "*Uggghhh!*"). Whatever online activities you endorse, insist that any internet material be age and situationally appropriate. Bonus points for stuff that makes you both laugh.

- Ask for advice on some small problem of your own. (*Hey, can you help me with a dilemma? My friend is hosting a party where she sells clothes to people, but I wouldn't wear that style of clothing. How do you think I can get out of going without hurting her feelings? Any suggestions for me on how to deal with that?*) Just make it real—kids are expert at sniffing out parental manipulation.

- Identify some hands-on repair or project only she can help you complete. Give yourself permission to break something for the sole purpose of getting her involved in constructive activity. Invite her to "coach" you and lead you through the process. Feeling focused, needed, and successful can be a huge mood-lifter—*if* you're able to get your kid to participate.

4. Communicate.

- Learn how to talk and listen in constructive ways (examples below). Communication is a beautiful, healing thing, and so is trust.

- Try to maintain an attitude of calm and respect while you hear her out—even if you're hearing unhinged thoughts or suicidal ideation, and starting to panic.

- If you're going to cry, do your best to hold it in till he's not with you—or turn away until you can pull yourself together. I know, it feels impossible. Just remind yourself that you may be his only safe ally. Above all, you want him to keep opening up to you!

- Resist being pulled into the emotional cyclone. Panic and anguish have a way of feeding off each other (I know this first-hand). It may be one of the hardest things you'll do as a parent, but work on presenting a matter-of-fact demeanor when he tells you that eating lunch in the middle school cafeteria is killing him from the inside out—and that, if you *really loved him* you would let him stay home for the rest of his life. The first part of the complaint may be true, figuratively speaking. But you need him at school while you work on solutions—unless he's truly unsafe there. By modeling calm and strength, you may well empower him to get through the day, rather than spiraling out of control with him.

- Be honest about the need for accessing immediate, professional help—tell him you'll have to call the doctor or the crisis team, or go to the ER if you can't keep him safe.
- Don't obsess over "objective facts" and engage in fruitless debate when she says things she may believe, but you know are not objectively true. (*I can't take the math SATs and I'll never go to college because I'm so dumb. Anyway, you can't get ahead in life if you don't take the math SATs and go to a good college so I'll be living here in this bedroom forever, and I can't even make money because you can't make a living if you don't pass the math SATs.*) She may be experiencing cognitive distortion—common in folks with severe mental health disorders—and it's not a battle worth having in the moment. Try to gently redirect her thinking without negating the truth of her feelings. It's not easy, but with practice, this is a learnable skill.
- Teach her the art and science of "detective thinking." This concept is widely used in therapeutic practices but can easily be employed at home by anyone with a child who needs a perspective reset.

Run through the following exercise with your child of any age who needs help managing unfounded worries. Talk him through it and have him speak his answers. An older kid can complete the exercise in writing once she's gotten the hang of it. If they can internalize it and use it independently as a strategy on the go, all the better.

DETECTIVE THINKING
What thought is troubling me right now?
Why is it troubling me?
Rate my anxiety between 0 and 10 (0 = none; 10 = extremely high).
What is the WORST that can happen?
List evidence for: List evidence against:
Is my *evidence for* reasonable?
Is my *evidence against* reasonable?
Rate my anxiety again (0–10).

5. Be present.

- Vulnerable kids are easy prey to online bullies and predators. Know her tech habits. Does she use a smartphone to access the world? A laptop or tablet? *Your* awareness of her devices will go a long way toward ensuring your child's safety at home.
- Be clued in to what she's reading/watching, and with whom she's talking—and let her know you're paying attention.
- If necessary, mandate a computer and phone check every so often . . . or just confiscate her tech devices. She'll hate you for it, of course! But I'm willing to bet you'd rather deal with anger and hurt feelings all around, than having your heart ripped out by its tender roots when something goes very wrong.
- Inattention provides an opening for disaster. Don't "check out" in the middle of your child's psychiatric meltdown by physically walking away or mentally shutting down, unless another safe adult is there to spell you. I get it: you need a break. So do I. So does every other person reading this book. Damn, we *deserve* a break! And when the time is right, we'll be justified in taking one. Until then, make sure you are physically present and mentally aware, because the moment you look away may be the moment your kid needed you most. Bad things can happen unexpectedly fast . . . and we don't always get a second try.

The sad truth is that parents like us rarely *do* catch a break, of any kind— and the rest of the world (*sometimes even the experts who treat our kids!*) can be maddeningly tone deaf to our desperation. It's more than OK to get pissed off, to vent to your network (you're beginning to see why you need one!), or to indulge in thoughts like *This. Is. So. Not. Fair.* It's not! You're entitled to these feelings—but you do need to pick yourself up and jump back into the fray. The young life of your own, beloved child depends on it.

WATCH, WAIT, HIDE THE KNIVES: ANNABELLA'S STORY

I asked Annabella, mom to two teenage daughters—an eighteen-year-old with no known mental health issues, and a sixteen-year-old who has rapid-cycling bipolar disorder, anxiety, and ADHD—how she manages life at home in Rhode Island, when things go haywire.

Annabella: What's ironic about this whole situation is that I'm a master's-level mental health clinician, and I was totally blindsided by Maggie's illness! First of all, my training's in marriage and family therapy—nothing as serious as what we live with now. And also, I think I was caught off guard because Maggie seemed quite "typical" until she hit fourteen. A little oversensitive, maybe, but nothing too alarming.

It started with a suicide attempt—she downed a full bottle of ibuprofen tablets. All my husband and I could think was, *Thank God she didn't go for the half-empty bottle of Percocet too!* Or my husband's blood pressure medication. We figured it was a one-off, irrational decision made at a time of high stress. We thought, *They'll fix her up, she'll come home from the hospital and go back to school, friends, sports.* As if she had a broken leg! We told her coach and teammates from her elite cheerleading team that she'd be back soon. Just give her a month or six weeks, and she'll be back to the old Mags.

That didn't happen. (Well, of course it didn't!) We've been living day to day—hour to hour—ever since. Four long-term hospitalizations in a little more than a year. Four! Are we OK? No. But we're fighters. I don't know where this goes next, but I know it's for life. And I know it's unfair.

You asked about keeping safe in the house. Can I tell you a story, first? Maggie's mostly managing high school right now, although we recently requested a later start, and it still takes everything she's got to make it through the day. I wake her in the morning, and sometimes I feel like I've got to treat her like a fragile doll, tiptoeing around her so I don't trigger a crisis.

Last Friday I couldn't get her out the door to school, which does sometimes happen, and is not always a fight a parent can (or should) win, in my opinion. Her dad was working from home, and she said she felt safe enough for me to go to my office and see my patients.

I texted her from my car on the way to work to see if she was doing OK, because with rapid-cycling bipolar, things can change on a dime. (Yeah, I know, you're not supposed to text while driving. Sometimes I don't have a way *not* to text while driving!)

She answered, "No."

I asked her what she needed.

She said, "I feel unsafe in the house." I didn't wait to call my husband. She needed me there. I canceled my morning appointments. My clients were good about it. But really, how many canceled appointments, how much lost income, can we take?

Still, she's my girl. I love her so much! If she can't do school, and she's not in the hospital, she's got to be home—and I'm going to be there with her.

When I got to her she begged me to take her to the hospital, so I knew it was serious. I suggested we try some other things—driving around together, getting something nice to eat. I needed to keep her home, because her older sister was graduating from high school the next day. (That's always the way with these things, isn't it?) I thought if I bought some time she might cycle on to a better place. It wouldn't be a long-term fix, but my other child had this huge milestone the next day, and we had to be there for her. I mean, what are we supposed to do?

That's the kind of dilemma people like us find ourselves in on a regular basis. How do you decide on the path that'll cause the least harm to the least number of people? How do you know for sure if choosing the hospital is the right choice, right now? And if you do, but your insurance company disagrees, well . . . that's a whole other sad situation.

But getting back to safety at home: I hide all sharp things. During a suicidal spell, we've been known to sit around the dinner table trying to cut our steak with butter knives, pretending nothing's out of the ordinary.

"And how was your day?" we say to each other, which is pretty ridiculous when you think about it. On the other hand, that is our "normal." I even hide the girls' razors. If my older daughter wants to shave her legs in the shower, she's got to come ask me, and I'll bring one out of the secret stash. When Maggie wants to shave but she's not stable, she'll have me sit in the bathroom while she showers. When she's ready, she asks for the razor. When she's finished, she hands it back. I'm stuck there till she's done.

That's one thing typical families don't understand: just because a kid feels like she's going to hurt herself doesn't necessarily mean she wants to die—but honestly, you never know for sure.

Our biggest worry is overdose. Because she already tried to kill herself with pills, I lock them up and hide them away. But honestly, when she's unsafe I just track her around the house. If she's awake forty-eight hours in a row, I'm awake too. I doubt she could get her hands on something dangerous, but I'm not taking any chances. That's one of the nightmarish things about living like this: not knowing for sure what happens next. (Read more about Annabella and Maggie in chapter 4.)

> Remember: your home is not as structured or well staffed as a hospital or residential treatment center, and it's never going to be. If you screw up, accept that you did so with loving intent. Don't devalue your parental love—it's the one thing you, alone, can offer your child, and it's priceless.

"I CAME SO CLOSE, IT SCARED ME!": JOHN'S STORY

John, a dad of three from New York, told me about his own struggles to keep calm on the home front when his youngest child, Tim, "broke down."

John: Well, I guess I never expected to have a mentally ill child. Looking back, I really shouldn't have been surprised, since I'm pretty sure my older brother has undiagnosed bipolar disorder. Also, I learned as a middle-aged man that my own clinical anxiety and depression were interfering with my ability to parent Tim and the girls like the dad they deserved and needed.

From the time he was two, Tim just rubbed me the wrong way. I loved him, but I really didn't understand him. He seemed to thrive on being contrary. I know now that's not true—he couldn't help it. But everything I asked of him, all my expectations, he did the opposite. And if I responded with the least irritation or emotion, it just got worse.

My wife was suffering; our relationship was suffering. She was so stressed and tired, wanting to help our son, whom she loved, we both did—and who broke down continuously—that there was nothing left. Our intimacy went away completely, for several years.

Sometimes, no matter how much I loved my kids when they were little ones, they just frustrated me. Tim, especially. Maybe deep inside I was afraid that he inherited some kind of madness from me. When he was out of control—screaming, refusing food and sleep, begging that we buy him this or that, 24/7, because he always seemed to need something to satisfy the hunger of his heart—I lost my cool. I'm not proud of it, but I did.

Usually, these explosions happened at home. We were stuck there, not much to do, and maybe my wife was out at the store or the kids were just in each other's faces. Tim would always do something hurtful to one of the girls—and probably they provoked it, but his response was usually so out of proportion! There was one incident I want to delete from my memory, because it makes me feel like a horrible jerk. I know he remembers it too—my wife told me he used to bring it up to his teachers and therapists, which was embarrassing and painful to her.

Anyway, what happened that day was he did something enraging (the fact that I can remember my response but not the action that caused it speaks volumes, right?), and I picked him up and held him by his feet over his bed, head down. I was yelling and he was screaming. I shook him a little before letting him drop. It hurts even saying the words, because I must have scared the hell out of him. I scared myself, I'll tell you that. I came so close to going over the edge that day! I remember thinking I could not be left alone at home with him, because I couldn't trust myself to react in an appropriate way anymore.

The line between utter frustration and violence is so miniscule. I can see how people who mean well accidentally cross over to abuse, and that is scary. For a few years after I tossed my kid on the bed I was fucking *terrified* I'd become one of those parents. I loved my child, and at the same time I was afraid I'd hurt him.

I've tried to apologize to Tim, but it took many years before I could even say the words. I love him, and always have. He's graduating high school this year, and I'm beyond proud of him. He received a diagnosis of bipolar 1 when he was fifteen, on top of his terrible anxiety disorder, but in spite of these challenges he's living a pretty good life, all things considered.

I was formally diagnosed with some mental health issues, myself, in the past few years. I have to credit my wife for insisting I get myself evaluated by a psychiatrist. I never thought I'd end up on psych meds, but that's where things stand now. With them, I can handle most of what life throws at me, without blowing up. I know I'm a better dad, for sure—and hopefully, a better husband.

Tim and I have made some really positive memories in the aftermath of that bad one. He's spent his high school years at a therapeutic boarding school, which gave us all some space to heal, but I totally look forward to when he comes home on weekends and school breaks. We have a good relationship, and we do a lot of things together now.

THINGS YOU CAN DO TO BRING DOWN
THE TEMPERATURE AT HOME

- *Stream a movie or television show.* You're at home for the day, the week, or just a few hours, whether you like it or not. Allow yourself to be transported to a place that is funnier or happier than your place—or just far, far away from it. Do it just for *you*, if your child is stable, occupied, and within surveilling distance for the moment. Or do it together with him, side by side! Watch the same movie on TV, or different ones on separate laptops. There can be tremendous therapeutic power in watching a screen if you watch the right kinds of things. (See "Making Peace with the TV: Our Story, Snapshot #4" later on in this chapter.)
- *Explore audiobooks.* Both Benjy and I have found that the mental clutter that can accompany severe depression and anxiety affects our ability to sit down and read. Listening, though, can be done while pacing, bathing, eating, coloring, sitting on the toilet, and

even drifting off to sleep. Again, any time spent lost in story is time *not* spent dwelling on obsessive fears, acting on destructive urges, aggressing, or retreating into isolation. In many cases, it can be splendid therapy and distraction.

- *Move!* No, don't relocate—just get moving at home. I know, it sounds so hokey. And you're tired, and you've got a kid who's imploding, or exploding, or catatonic. If you're like me, exercise is number 299 on your 300-item to-do list. *But.* I'm talking about moving, not exercise, per se. Fire up your Spotify and dance. It's no big secret that music and movement, separately and together, can be huge mood lifters.[1] At the pediatric psych unit where Ben lived, for weeks at a time, as a repeat patient, the staff would pop a dance program into the Wii every night, and work through tricky routines with any kid who wanted to participate. That was a win for everyone! (By the way, for the "never-dancers" among us, a trampoline—used safely and with supervision—can serve the same purpose. Jumping has both physiological and emotional benefits.)
- *Take things outdoors—if and when you can.* You probably don't need convincing that a dip into nature's sounds, touches, and colors, however brief, is a healthful thing. If getting out is easier said than done—and sometimes it will be—just remind yourself and your child that there's a lot to see and do out there! Even the humblest garden stone guards its own secrets underneath. Explore the hidden spaces in your yard or on your street. Snap photos of bugs; watch squirrels and birds live their lives. Challenge each other to a game of Nature I Spy, or to guess the "facts of life" of any animal or vegetable species you encounter. Then go inside to look them up and see how you did.
- *Get calm—literally!* The Calm app (also available on the web) will take you to a zone where lapping waves, birdsong, and other sounds and visuals can offer you meditative peace. Mindful meditation is used increasingly in school and therapeutic settings, because it really works. Calm, like the similar apps and websites listed in chapter 1, provides the audio, video, and guidance; you just bring you—and anyone else in the family you can convince to join in.
- *Try the candles/aromatherapy/yoga route.* You may want to leave this for a last resort, if you think it's a bunch of new-age malarkey. I think it has the same potential as anything else you might try—and for some, these user-friendly, at-home therapies make a real difference.
- *Don't underestimate the power of water.* This may not work for an adolescent who's acting or feeling unsafe, because you can't fully

supervise them, but a long, hot shower or bath (scents and bubbles optional)? Well, that just speaks for itself, doesn't it? Not suitable, obviously, where medically or commonsensically prohibited—and you'll have to wait for yours until you've been relieved of duty by an appropriate adult.

- *Put on some classical music.* It has been argued that a daily dose of Mozart can squelch depression.[2] Avoid angsty, thunderous, and atonal stuff. Music by composers like Mozart, Haydn, or Bach would be a good choice. (An older kid may make the choice for you with a resounding *No way!* to classical music of any kind.) Even if you try it and notice no real difference in anyone's mental health, you still get to listen to some beautiful music. There's something to be said for absorbing the beauty in our world, every chance we get!

- *Allow your kid (and you) to use food for comfort.* I'm bracing myself for backlash from the nutrition and wellness communities, but I'll say it anyway: if need be, forget the green stuff today and go straight for the chocolatey, the crisp-and-salty, the sweet-and-carby. Now, I don't suggest this as a long-term strategy; experts tend to agree that what we eat, in general, has a direct effect on how we feel and function. I can attest to this myself. And let's not forget that our kids are already at risk for weight gain if they're taking psych meds. On the other hand, you gotta do what you gotta do.

- *Just because a solution seems obvious doesn't mean it's not worth trying.* Are you rolling your eyes at "bubble baths" and "chocolate"? Yes? Give these a try before giving up. Why? Because, *what if they work?* They're a cheap and easy fix—even if a temporary one. Why *wouldn't* you try them out? You can always use a few new tools in the ol' parenting toolbox.

BELIEVE IT OR NOT . . .

Places that seem perfectly safe to you (for example, your own home) may be hotbeds of stress and fear for your teenager.

"Teen brains rely on early-maturing brain structures that process fear differently than adult brains, according to an NIMH-funded study. As a result, teens may have more difficulty than adults in differentiating between danger and safety, leading to more pervasive stress and anxiety."[3]

Digital and Hands-On Resources

So far you've encountered suggestions in this chapter on promoting safety, improving communication, creating distraction, and etching that critical "home plan" into your frazzled mind. You've read a list of tactics to try when disorder is on the rise and you're with your kid at home. So far, so good.

But what about specifics? Where and who are these parents like you, who "get" you and can offer comfort and advice on demand—even when you're housebound? What hands-on, physical things can your child—and you—do at home? And are there recommended stories to read, hear, and/ or watch—solo or together? All of these resources exist. You can find them, and start making them work for you.

TAP INTO THE COMMUNITIES OF FACEBOOK

If you've got a computer and internet access, you can join Facebook for free. The things many folks use the platform for—reconnecting with old friends; posting vacation pics, recipes, political rants; and so on—are completely optional, and probably best avoided if you're in a fragile emotional place. The best (and also the worst, but that's a topic for another day) aspects of Facebook are its communities of like-minded people.

Use the search bar on Facebook to find your tribe(s) and the virtual spaces they hang out in. (In my case, these include groups for families of kids with mental health challenges in my state, and for parents of "quirky kids"; regional and national mental health information groups; special education groups; and some writing, virtual yard sale, and gardening groups— because we can't live only for the hard stuff, right?) Once you've found them, join them!

For starters, your local school district's Special Education Parent Advisory Council (SEPAC) may have a Facebook page for members. These are parents of kids with emotional, physical, or intellectual differences who receive special education services. (If not, they'll occupy a corner of real estate on your school district's website; grab the group leaders' contact info and reach out.) And those SEPAC folks may form a basis for your network of fellow mental health parents. Chat them up, ask for referrals, resources, introductions to people in *their* networks. Keep going from there. Networks function kind of like compound interest: your initial "investment" will grow on its own—and with some replenishment on your part, your web of connections will expand exponentially.

If you need help creating effective search terms for finding Facebook groups, my discussion of "diagnostic Googling" in chapter 1 demonstrates strategies for searching smart.

Check Out Some Mental Health and Related Blogs

BLUE LIGHT BLUE
(HTTP://BLUELIGHTBLUE.COM/)

This is one of the most powerful blogs I've ever read—on any subject. Its creator, Amy McDowell Marlow, is a "20-year survivor of suicide loss who lives with mental illness—major depression, generalized anxiety disorder and PTSD." What can I say, beyond *Read this, ASAP?* You'll be glad you did.

Pros: Raw, honest, and uplifting. Amy McDowell Marlow exemplifies "survivor." If she's the face of severe mental illness, then we have all kinds of reasons to feel hopeful.

Cons: As with any personal account of serious human suffering, parts of this blog can be tough to read.

A STORIED MIND
(HTTPS://WWW.STORIEDMIND.COM/)

With such a great name, how could this blog not offer sensitive and powerful personal insights into the author's experience with depression? It's not geared toward childhood mental illness, but just in case the apple hasn't fallen far from the tree—or you're thinking ahead to your depressed kid's adult life—it's totally worth a long look.

Pros: Really helpful if you're feeling lost, lonely, or worried about sheer survival. I love the fact that, along with talking about his own life with depression, the author devotes substantial space to other people's "recovery stories"—told by them, in the first person, much like the parent stories included in this book. But you'll also find discussions of recent research, therapeutic options, and links to useful resources.

Cons: A Storied Mind is not explicitly about parenting children with depression—but that's not really a con, since you've got this book and other resources to fill that need. It's honest, which means reading it can be depressing in and of itself—but sooner or later we've all got to face the facts, even the hard ones. You might save this for later if your child struggles with psychiatric conditions other than depression, and you're looking for a more topical blog. Although, for the record, it's likely that *any* serious illness will bring depression along for the ride—even if the depression is secondary and only intermittent.

A DAY IN OUR SHOES
(HTTPS://ADAYINOURSHOES.COM/)

Lisa Lightner, disability parent and professional advocate extraordinaire, will either make you feel like a budding superhero (yes, she is that inspiring), or a complete slacker (yes, she is that *impossibly* energetic, brave, and determined). Either way, if you're parenting a child with significant psychiatric involvement, then you are—or should be—parenting a kid on an IEP, otherwise known as an Individualized Education Plan. (Got no idea what an IEP is? Start reading *A Day in Our Shoes* now! If school poses a challenge due to his or her illness, your child is going to need one.)

Pros: How best to say it? Lisa Lightner takes the boulders life flings at her and her family and chisels them into tools. There is so much to learn here, and loads of inspiration—even for veteran disability parents. It's a great place to read up on your child's rights under federal special education law, learn how to deal with a difficult school district (or an easygoing one—because, hey, those exist. So do unicorns, right?), and explore ways to advocate on a larger scale.

Cons: Good grief! You've slept twelve hours and showered once in the past week, and some blogger who probably showers every day wants you to improve your IEP game *and* call your senators and representatives today? I know. This blog may be best left for those times when all's quiet on the home front, you're not driving across the universe and back for medical and therapy appointments, and your cortisol spikes are down to a mere couple per week. Also, best avoided when you're bogged down in self-doubt or self-loathing—unless you're easily inspired.

PSYCHOLOGY TODAY BLOGS
(WWW.PSYCHOLOGYTODAY.COM)

The website of the famous magazine features a plenitude of blogs by experts in their fields of psychology/therapy. Some topics are sexier than others. (The ones of primary interest to readers of this book are fairly unsexy, but there's some excellent advice doled out in them.) Search by topic to find what you need. You might even bump into my own blog: *What to Expect When You Get the Unexpected: A Mother's Notes on Childhood Mental Illness.*

THE STRIPED NICKEL

(WWW.THESTRIPEDNICKEL.BLOGSPOT.COM)

This was my personal blog, begun at the time of Benjy's first inpatient hospitalization, and retired around three years later. Read it if you'd like to spend a few minutes, here and there, in the company of a family somewhat like yours. Here's a random entry that reminds me how much *I didn't know yet* while I was writing it—and how challenging living day to day with an unquiet mind can be:

> Benjy is an odd mix of self-confident and self-despising (more often the latter). Today when I picked him up from his therapeutic day school he piled into the car, glowing, and said, "I ran a lap around the courtyard in TWENTY SECONDS!!"
>
> "Wow," I said. "That's good."
>
> "Yeah," he said. "I'm a good runner. I think I can run about 15 miles per hour. Is that really fast?"
>
> I had no idea, but I told him it was.
>
> He continued, "I run with these tiny steps, like Sonic, and I'm about as fast as him, too. My legs are a blur."
>
> Sonic is a video game character. I presume he is a fast runner.
>
> When Benjy has an inflated sense of his own abilities I usually go with it—not because I want to raise a kid who is "the best" at everything (a lot of people seem to subscribe to this parenting philosophy), but because it makes me happy to see him feeling good about himself. His more frequent attitude is, I'm the worst, I'm worthless, don't waste your time with me.
>
> Recently we've been seeing this other Ben. This excessively confident child. And what we haven't seen as much of are the self-inflicted injuries that accompany his off-kilter cycles. When his body is tight with anxiety, and his is mind, too; when he is suffused with sadness and self-loathing, his body exists only to be battered and insulted. Even my caresses can't drive off those cruel impulses.
>
> But it's been weeks since I've seen any of that, except for one compulsive strike—biting his lower lip bloody. Otherwise it's been peaceful around here, and his body has been healing. The last hair-raising episode I can remember was when he was in the hospital, back in October, and

taped a sheet of paper with a bulls-eye and the words "Shoot Here" to his forehead. That was not a good day for Lars and me. It was definitely not a good day for Ben.

Here, in our peculiar corner of the universe, we take things one day at a time. It's a bit less stressful, and less devastating, that way. As it turns out, this day has been a pretty good one. It's Saskia's 14th birthday, Benjy is a Runner, and I am sitting nearby them, listening to them enjoy each other's company. It was only a month ago that we were in as bad a place as I could have imagined (okay, maybe not quite as bad—I have a crazy imagination). And now, things are so much better—not the "normal" other people know, but better for us—I could cry.

Boot Up Your Electronics: TV/Movies/Documentaries

There's lot of distraction to be found on TV, or streamed on your devices. Your local public library may also have just what the doctor ordered, on DVD or even videotape. Try the BBC's *Planet Earth* (multiple episodes), for kids of any age and mental health status: if they're able to sit and focus, there's something there to divert their attention. You'll love it too. Just be forewarned: the occasional predator/prey dance ends badly for the underdog.

What's going to resonate with your kid and family is a personal call. Expect trial and error, and make sure to ask among your growing network of mental health families for their suggestions.

Audiobooks

AUDIBLE (BY AMAZON)

Makes book consumption convenient and portable. Are you resistant to reading this way? I was, but it turned out to be easier than books on tape/CD, and more practical, given how we live around here, than physical books. You don't necessarily have to shell out bucks for an audiobook—or an e-book, either, if you enjoy reading on a laptop or tablet. Most public libraries lend them to anyone with a library card, just like books made of paper. Better yet, the whole transaction can be completed online, with you in your birthday suit—if that's what floats your boat.

BLINKIST

I love this app, because it opens a window on all those nonfiction books I've been wanting to read but will never, ever have the time or attention span for. It distills the books into "blinks," or topical units (you can listen to these or read them), so you get the gist in about fifteen minutes without committing to the whole—unless you decide, after Blinkist, you want to go for the grown-up version.

Get Your Hands on Some Therapeutic Activities

COLORING BOOKS

Coloring isn't only for little kids anymore! There's a coloring book out there for everyone in the family . . . and you can even download free pages from the internet. (Just Google, baby!)

You probably know people who own adult coloring books, along with the usual child-focused products. Their pervasive presence in hospitals, libraries, and stores of all stripes suggests that the act of coloring holds some therapeutic value in our anxietized culture. Try it out—maybe this is the day that coloring becomes the antidote to your kid's emotional dysregulation (and the sedative you wish you could take, but can't, when your sky is falling down).

PAT A BUNNY!

Or a dog, or a cat . . . or a chinchilla. It doesn't matter what species of warm, furry creature grants you the gift of therapy. Just know that living with a pet can reduce anxiety, bring down blood pressure, and simply make you feel happier. Yes, there's research to prove it,[4] not to mention a ton of anecdotal evidence suggesting the health-giving properties of furry housemates.

WHEN YOU JUST *CAN'T* ANYMORE AND NEED A SCHEDULED BREAK? TRY RESPITE SERVICES

A common theme of this survival guide is the acute or chronic stress suffered by families of young people with serious mental health disorders, and what to do about it. One resource that can help frazzled parents recharge is known as "respite care." Respite care can be inside or outside the home, and involves temporarily handing over your supervisory duties to a qualified caregiver. These services can sometimes be arranged and paid for by one of your state's social service agencies. As with most things in life, buyer beware—but if you manage to find the right match for your kid and your family, respite care can make a huge impact on your quality of life!

Trying out respite services can be scary. For *our* first foray into respite we hired a college student named Holly, a young woman majoring in early childhood education, to watch our very young kids for ten hours per week. We didn't know what it was called; we only knew that our family was sinking, and that my father's oldest friend, Leon Hammer, insisted my parents help us pay for regular child care before I grew seriously ill from stress. (See chapter 1 for more on Dr. Hammer and how he taught me about valuing myself.) Holly's assistance was life restoring to me—respite, in the truest sense. In those precious ten hours each week, I wrote for my very life—fiction, poetry, all kinds of doodles, and lists upon lists upon lists. (Lists make me feel more secure.)

It wasn't easy entrusting Benjy to anyone who wasn't us, no matter how desperate we were for a break. After Holly moved on, the closest we got to a real break was the rare evening out, when we'd enlist my brother and sister-in-law, or hire a babysitter. My biggest regret from those years? We should have gifted ourselves some respite more often.

PARENT Q&A: USING RESPITE CARE
FOR HELP ON THE HOME FRONT

I spoke with Pam L., mom to two sons, about her experiences with respite services:

DV: Why did you choose to seek respite from parenting your child?
PL: To give myself and my youngest child a chance to rest and regain energy.

DV: Did you opt for respite in your home or in another space—and why choose one over the other?
PL: I have had both in-home and out-of-home respite. I think they are both very valuable. If I had to choose, I would choose in-home because I know my child is still in a place of comfort.

DV: What did you do while responsibility for your child was briefly shifted to someone else?
PL: I would just relax and spend time with my other child. As an only parent (my husband passed away 8 years ago), it is crucial that I

recharge my batteries. If I am completely overwhelmed, stressed, and "done," then I'm not able to help my son the way I want to.

DV: How did you feel the first time you tried using respite?
PL: I was both scared and relieved. I felt very guilty, but also desperate to get a break.

DV: How difficult was it to find reliable and qualified respite providers—and were you satisfied with them?
PL: It was very difficult to find in-home respite providers. I had to find my own through Care.com. We tried using an agency suggested by my state's mental health agency, but the people they sent were not qualified. One guy even put my son on YouTube!

DV: Did you have any especially positive respite experiences you'd like to share?
PL: The girl I found on Care.com was a wonderful help to my family. She even went on to major in special education and wants to be a BCBA (board-certified behavioral analyst) because of my son!

DV: How would you recommend other parents find a respite provider if they decide to try it?
PL: I think the best respite provider would be a college student going to school for special education, teaching, nursing, etc. The state mental health agencies should work with the local colleges. It's great experience for them, and it's a lifesaver for us!

A Few Suggestions for Locating Respite Caregivers:

- Tap your local school district, college/university, or child care center for teachers, students, or professional caregivers looking for some extra work.
- Contact your state's Department of Health and Human Services for information on programs that might connect families with respite workers or therapeutic mentors (whose job is to take your kid out into the community for a bit of life-skills practice and some fun, while giving you an hour off).
- Work your personal and online communities for referrals to qualified respite providers. You know you need those networks!

MAKING PEACE WITH THE TV:
OUR STORY, SNAPSHOT #4

I was such a snob before life whacked me upside the head.

I spent my pre-motherhood, adult life as a literary scholar. I mostly read stuff written before the twentieth century, preferably on another continent. My television tasting menu consisted of one item: PBS. My typical film wish list: 10 Art Flicks, 0 Other.

I know, I know. I was the worst kind of high-culture snob. Not that I didn't love that high-art stuff. It filled me with buoyancy and light. It still does, on the rare occasions I indulge in it. We just have a conflicted, on-and-off relationship.

Why's that? I had kids. Life got harder. I did read Shakespeare's *The Tempest* aloud to my week-old Saskia, because I feared that, as a mother, I would lose connection with my old intellectual life. Just a few short years later, our family began weathering one explosive crisis after another.

More than once, it was our trusty TV that saved us from those raging storms.

With Benjy, what worked best in his childhood and preteen years was anything that involved animals, history, or science. The BBC's *Planet Earth* was a perennial favorite. If a nature video was narrated by the British naturalist David Attenborough, it had decent odds of tamping down whatever emotional surge was drowning Ben in the moment. Dinosaur documentaries could sometimes get the job done (at a certain point he knew everything about everything prehistoric). As Ben got older, we could both get lost in video reproductions of famous tank battles from World War II, or iconic World War I Allied versus Axis dogfights. I watched so many of these things by his side, at a certain point I knew everything about everything that was knocking about in my son's brain.

Except the irregular stuff, which is confoundingly hard to know.

The thing is, the simple act of losing ourselves in some engrossing story was sometimes enough to give us a break. Even a short one of those quiet spells can make a world of difference—for parent *and* child. If it works for one in five tries, then it's worth it. True, urging your kid to join you in watching some show could escalate a host of problems. You'll know soon enough if it's going to help.

Don't limit your use of screen time to tempering immediate crises. I learned by accident that bonding over a shared TV experience could mend an assortment of parent-child rifts. Take my relationship with Saskia, for example: it wasn't until Benjy left home for a residential school the next state over that I realized how ragged it had become. She was angry, anxious, depressed. I'd never noticed because one kid with emotional dysregulation was my limit. Without Ben present, ever poised on the brink of the grave, I could focus directly on Saskia. Her neediness was quieter than her brother's, but no less urgent.

Saskia and I had some major work to do. Lucky for us, we had a TV, a comfy yellow couch, and hundreds of channels to surf.

One evening she invited me to sit down beside her and watch some reality TV—the kind of show I would have scorned previously. I started to say, "Thanks, no thanks—" but something made me say yes instead.

I'm glad I did. That Bad TV *was so good*. For her, for me, for us. Shows like *My Big Fat Gypsy Wedding* and *I Wanna Marry Harry* healed the rift that had opened between us. We bonded, laughing together at the embarrassing antics of these people. We sat ever closer on the couch, Saskia inching over until she came close enough to lay her head on my shoulder, then burrowing into that warm space beneath my encircling arm. Somehow, watching these shows made us feel better about ourselves. They gave us a guilty pleasure to anticipate every night after supper—the time of day when Ben's absence hit us most intensely.

OPEN MIC: KIDS SPEAK OUT!

Aimee, Age Nineteen (New Mexico)

When my sister was suicidal the whole house was stressed out. My mom would be trying to fix everything—my sister, me and my health issues (I had a lot of weird symptoms when I was in middle school, though the doctors never figured me out), financial issues, and her own health issues. My dad would spend extra time at work, probably to get away from us. Our family was kind of broken, I guess.

It made me incredibly anxious, watching my mom follow Alyssa all around the house, walking on eggshells so she didn't say the wrong thing and set her off. She didn't worry as much about saying the right things to me. Not that I wanted any of her focus. Sometimes they'd wake me at 2 a.m. to say, "Don't worry, it's all okay, but we're taking Aly to the hospital. If we're not here when you wake up, call Ginger [Mom's friend] and she'll come over." I never knew, when I went to sleep, whether I'd be woken up to my sister in full meltdown mode, my mom frantically talking to the psychiatrist and my dad trying to calm her down and packing up her clothes. Or if I'd wake up all alone in the house.

This whole situation started when I was around eleven.

When home was depressing or stressful I read books. My favorite series, Percy Jackson, I read probably eight times, cover to cover, in a couple years' time. I'd pretend I lived in Percy's universe rather than my own. It was the best escape in the world.

I used movies and TV series in the same way. There were a lot of places I'd rather be than home, where there was so much emotional upheaval—my baby sister growing into this stranger, unrecognizable, and my mom looking like she carried the weight of all our broken pieces on her back. Both my parents arguing and unhappy. They loved us and they still do. I am starting to see, now, from an adult's perspective, what it must have been like for them. That makes me sad.

I do have my own anxiety and depression, only not as severe as Aly's. Stuff like that gets worse when your world feels out of control. Sometimes home feels even more crazy than the outside world. It's like, I love my family and my home. I *want* them to be "normal" and happy. Of course, that's out of my hands. If I had that kind of power . . . well, I wish!

What I can do for myself is find a way to reinvent my life. Books, TV, movies. I write too. I'm nineteen now, and I still use those means of escape. I have my certain places at home: my bedroom, a corner of our attic by the dormer window, the TV room, which can be closed off and made pitch dark.

I also use weed to curb my anxiety when it gets out of control. It definitely takes the edge off. I started getting high somewhat regularly in my last year of high school, because my inner turmoil got too intense. I continued with the weed into college. It's probably not what any parent would want to hear, but it really helps me push through.

THE TAKEAWAY

In General

- Your child in the throes of psychiatric crisis can engage in dangerous behaviors—at any age.
- Being at home with your kid-in-crisis is usually a surmountable challenge—but it is often devastatingly *hard*.
- Home can be a fortress or a minefield.

- Make sure, as you guide your child and family across the minefield, to look after yourself too.

The Specifics

- Play it safe: hide the sharps and other dangerous stuff.
- Practice smart supervision.
- Communicate and listen in positive, empowering ways.
- Make a home plan—and use it!
- Consider animal therapy.
- Seek respite—and use the break however you need to. Write, sleep, organize, shop, sneak out on a flash date, hang out with your other kids, or anything else that fills your well.
- Do what it takes to de-escalate a bad situation. Even resorting to the tactics on a "normal" parent's blacklist—like Bad TV, junk food, and bribery—is better than a fretful, sleepless night, at home or in the emergency room.

3

WHEN YOU MUST GET
OUT AND ABOUT

For better or for worse, life requires us to spend time in public. It may take a tremendous effort to get out there and face the world when adversity is nipping at your flanks. I've been there. I've calculated how sitting at home would be slightly easier than the weekly, eight-mile drive to therapy with a panicked, manic, or suicidal kid who was dead set against that eight-mile drive to therapy. I've dreamed up clever excuses for canceling pretty much anything at the last minute—even my *own* things, like going out with friends or to the gym, because stepping outside my ever-contracting world was too damned hard.

I've made these decisions well aware that the consequence (for us both) would just be more isolation and sadness, on top of what we started with. Or that I'd end up shadowing Ben all day long, stress-eating junk food, and peeing with the door open until another set of eyes and ears arrived home. I made similar choices for myself alone, when I was still trying to hold down a job while keeping my family from imploding—declining the occasional party or lunch invitation from colleagues, skipping the yearly end-of-semester faculty celebrations. What could I possibly talk about with *them*? It would have been easier to swallow live goldfish than schmooze about stuff that had become only superficially relevant to my life. Illness, disorder, and sleep deprivation? Those I could go on and on about—but I'd learned quickly that most people don't want to hear it.

I'm not proud of all that opting out, but I still do it now, when I am depleted of will and energy. I'm guessing you do too. Who wouldn't? Yet opting out is not a sustainable life strategy, even when life is totally disordered. It simply reinforces the idea that whatever exists on the other side of the front door is monstrous—which justifies our fear of stepping out.

Reader, that is one cycle of crazy you do not want to get into. I did, and it took me years to claw my way out.

I wish I'd figured out some decent *escape plans* from the get-go. I use the term "escape plan" in these pages to mean both "escaping a bad situation and returning to comfort," and its apparent opposite: "getting out of the cocoon and into the world." Confused? Don't be. Remember, *home* is not always synonymous with *comfort* for parents like us, nor is *discomfort* ever completely avoidable. Think of the escape plan as a strategy that gets you to the place you need to be, when you need to be there. Sometimes that's home. Sometimes it's school, or Aunt Irene's Tupperware party, or work. Occasionally it's "anywhere but here."

At times you will think, *Nope, we can't get there from here.* The truth is, with an escape plan at the ready, you probably can.

Like the home plan I discussed in the previous chapter, escape plans require hard-won experience. You can't create successful methods of getting yourself and your child where you need to be without some trial and error. And because what works for one child at one moment might not work for the very same child at another moment (let alone work for *your* child, ever), you can learn only so much from reading before you've got to start doing. This chapter will help you get going.

FIVE THINGS I WISH I KNEW FROM THE BEGINNING

1. You're not the only parent who's imagined smacking another person's kid upside the head, after witnessing that kid taunting yours at the playground. It's normal. Indulge in the image, and move on.
2. Don't let people who don't know or understand you make you and your family feel unwelcome in the community. Public spaces belong to all of us equally.
3. Seclusion can fuel depression, and depression is catching. When chronic sadness spreads through your family (and it surely will, if you've got even one child with a serious mental illness), everything gets harder for everyone. So, focus on getting the gang out of the house, singly or all together.
4. As a general rule, you are the person most likely to be forgotten. Make sure you get your own break from the emotional chaos at home.
5. The least sliver of opportunity is worth snatching. Even the briefest pause—a walk around the block, a cup of tea and five minutes of

silence on your front stoop—can change your outlook from dim to bright(er).

CLOSE ENCOUNTERS OF THE PUBLIC KIND

Imagine one of these scenes:

1. You desperately need to slip out to 7-Eleven for a six-pack of toilet paper. Your teenager, home on a day pass from the hospital, is ignoring your suggestions he join you for the outing. If you leave him unsupervised, you'll break every rule of good parenting *and* violate the conditions under which you signed him out today. The situation is urgent: paper towels definitely clog the toilet.
2. Your daughter with bipolar disorder is trending manic, just in time for her siblings' soccer and drama practices—and your significant other is at a job interview with the phone on silent mode. The pull in opposite directions feels like it's gonna kill you.
3. Your ten-year-old is begging you, for the umpteenth time, to go bowling. Even though you were *not* born yesterday—you know that with every gutter ball comes the prospect of an epic emotional eruption—you can't deflect forever! I mean, how many viable excuses can one human parent make up? (Fewer than a hundred. In all likelihood, maybe twenty?)

Pick any of the above—the end game is the same. You really do have to get out of your house, and often you really will have at least one emotionally vulnerable kid with you. Readers, these are the times that try parents' souls . . . and they're inescapable.

School and work are nonnegotiable—except when our kids can't do school. Ditto for basic obligations such as dental appointments, family events, and stepping out to restock the empty fridge. These are everyday pieces of a typical family's life. But "everyday" and "typical" are as meaningless, in our world, as "nonnegotiable." What is life with mental illness but an interminable series of negotiations with the typical, the expected, the necessary?

When there are other kids in the picture, whose needs and schedules conflict with those of your emotionally challenged child, you will always find the number of adults able and willing to choreograph this dance with you to be insufficient.

So, what can you do when you simply *must* get out that door, with one or more kids and multiple agendas to juggle? Have an escape plan up your sleeve.

Preparation Is Everything

You may have laughed bitterly just now, when you read the words "have an escape plan up your sleeve." I get it—I'm laughing mirthlessly with you as I reread them. When you regard eight minutes of calm as a major triumph, and your memory of the last time you read a book or went out with friends or had sex with your partner is hazy at best, you just don't want to hear advice like "Plan an escape." Especially on those days it feels like there *will be no escape, ever.*

Still, I stand by my statement. You may not be able to do it now. After all, we can only do as much as our inner and outside resources permit. This process of forming your escape plan could take a year. For me, it took about ten long, slow ones. My eventual cache of strategies was not the outcome of any conscious, strategic endeavor, but a subconscious buildup of lived experience. At some point I noticed I had these valuable coping mechanisms up my sleeve, and started using them to get us where we needed to go, and back to a safe(r) place when things went steeply downhill in public spaces.

So, how do you get started on your conscious or subconscious escape planning? There's no silver bullet—not that I've found, anyway. What you can do, and probably do every day already, is develop a deeper understanding of your child, yourself, and your family dynamic. This will likely evolve in fits and starts—and as our kids are more prone than the average child to be in flux, the plan you come up with may need frequent retooling. Eventually, you'll learn to tap into your deeper understanding to help you and your child navigate the outside world, just as you do on the home front.

Admittedly, this is not an intuitive practice for all parents. If you're like me, panic and desperation are the usual when faced with wrangling a dysregulated child or teen out the door and into some public space. For many years, I summoned my mechanical alter ego, the "MomBot," when I couldn't face the challenges of school refusal, food refusal, leaden despondency, suicidal ideation, and manic irritability on my own. She served her purpose and kept us going—with all the nuance of a bulldozer. In other words, I did not deal strategically or deliberately with these situations in the early days (no, wait—*decade*!) of Benjy's illness. I didn't even know exactly what was happening until we had an accurate diagnosis around the age of twelve. I just gritted my bot-teeth and slogged my way through every bipolar crisis, until my energy flagged, or my resolve weakened.

If your only available mode is MomBot or DadBot mode, don't worry about it. Do what you must to keep everyone in one piece, and to maintain some forward momentum. Once you have the capacity to think things through and prep in advance for these difficult moments, you will feel more in control when your kid's mental/emotional status begins to spiral—at home or out in public. That's the beauty of the escape plan.

SORRY, THERE'S NO MAGIC BULLET

- *Don't expect* to sit down tomorrow night after everyone's asleep and map out a direct path to Everything Is Ok. It takes time to discard the conventional wisdom about parenting, and learn how *your* kid needs and deserves to be parented.
- *Do remember* that no escape plan—or parenting strategy in general—is one size fits all. This is especially true when your kid has a mental health disorder. Schizophrenia is not bipolar disorder is not OCD is not reactive attachment disorder, and so on. Take the advice doled out in this chapter and entire book as a starting point—a sketch you'll fill in with your own paints.

Start Defining Your Escape Routes and Routines

Begin the process by asking yourself a few pointed questions. I recommend a written or audio-recorded list at this stage, if you can find some time and space to make one. Eventually your collection of usable escape plans will be cataloged in your brain, much like the home plan discussed in chapter 2, but the process of writing down your Q&As or talking yourself through them can be helpful in these early stages.

Start by looking at the big picture.

1. *Where do you (and your family) need or want to go?* When Benjy was at his most disabled by mood and anxiety disorders, *my* list, for example, would have included:
   - Work
   - School

- Grocery shopping
- Violin lessons
- Doctors/therapists
- Vet
- School events
- Writing group
- Playgrounds
- Sibling concerts
- Family gatherings
- Clothes/supplies shopping

2. *Are there alternative "routes" to some of your* must-go *places, just in case?* While the whole point of this chapter is *You've gotta get out into the world, despite all the crap the world dumps on your head*, it's crucial that you make the *right choice for right now*.

Every time you consider taking your son or daughter out with you, pause, breathe, and ask yourself: *Is this outing necessary?* And then: *Is our destination a trap* at this moment? If rising storms make leaving the house impossible, try taking a detour to get you (virtually) to your destination. (You will find links to some of these "detours/escape resources" later on in the chapter.)

- *Work:* If your work typically occurs outside your home, consider these options when an emotional crisis means you just can't get there in the flesh:

  - *See if you can telecommute.* This is only appropriate if you can actually accomplish work in the eye of an emotional hurricane. Faking it, while in truth you're desperately Googling various psychiatric disorders and leaving weepy messages on the clinician's emergency line, has a low rate of success. Trust me, I know.
  - *Use your PTO (paid time off).* This may seem obvious, but do you actually do it? If your employer offers *paid time off—a total pool of workdays that can be taken as sick, personal, and/or vacation days*—for Pete's sake, use it when you need it! I know that, in the U.S. at any rate, there can be risks associated with being nervy enough to *use* your earned PTO and not seeming a "team player." And yes: that is utterly crazy, heartless stuff. But right now your choices are limited—and they all stink. It's your call whether you disclose the real reasons you need your paid time off. (For more on disclosure, read on!)

○ *Learn your rights under FMLA (The Family and Medical Leave Act).* Some workers (dependent on size of employer and length of employment) are *legally entitled* to unpaid family leave to care for a sick family member. Yes, it's a flawed solution. You need the money, and if you take time off without pay to deal with a child's mental health crisis, you're just inviting financial grief into your life. But mental illness in your family is going to drain your resources anyway. Utilizing FMLA may just be one of those lesser-of-two-evils situations. At least you're protected from being fired if your child needs your complete (temporary) focus.

○ *Have an honest conversation with your boss about what's happening in your life.* Like taking time off, this carries some risk, but you never know—she or he could have a heart. It's worth asking the people in your mental health networks how *they* handle work-related (or other) conflicts. Even if they can't tell you what to do and how to do it, they'll be some of your best sources of information and moral support.

• *Shopping:*

○ *Buy online.* If you're organized enough to think ahead—or it's not an urgent need—why not try it? You can shop online for clothing, school/office supplies, pet supplies, groceries, and almost anything else you can think of. It's not always the most cost-effective solution—and for most of us, cost matters, because money is perpetually tight—but if you have your wits about you, *it is actually possible to spend less by shopping online.*

• *Therapy:*

○ *Go virtual.* Arrange for therapy via phone or videoconference. It's worth asking; lots of therapists offer this option nowadays. (Even basic medical care via teleconference is becoming more widely available.)

• *Your daily chores and errands:*

○ *Barter, wheedle, trade.* Asking for help can be so hard. But if you learn to do it, your life may become easier. Out of milk for breakfast cereal, and the resultant row looks like it's going to be a showstopper? "Borrow" a bowl's worth from a neighbor. (I've once or twice sent a kid, Pyrex measuring cup in hand, to knock on a neighbor's door and request a cup of milk

MANAGING WORK AND MENTAL ILLNESS?
DONNA HARDAKER MODELS A "NEW NORMAL"

In an inspirational personal essay, "Speaking Up for a New Normal,"[1] Hardaker, a Toronto-based workplace mental health consultant, describes her decision to disclose her own mental illness at work. Her take on why it was imperative to do so is relevant to those of us once-removed from the experience of mental illness too: parents, adult children, siblings, or partners of a loved one whose illness may impact our work. Hardaker writes:

> I have times of illness and times of wellness. When I am unwell I am afraid that the symptoms will never go away. Yet I do get better, in a constant process of recovery and growth. Like many of [the more than six million Canadians who live with a psychiatric disorder], I have experienced loss due to mental illness. I lost a job and a career. I almost lost my life. Yet I am one of the very fortunate ones who had the resources and the support to re-invent myself. My career now involves raising awareness about mental health issues in the workplace. I stand in front of thousands of people every year and say the words: "I have a mental illness."
>
> I have "come out" at work. I have told my employer that I have a mental illness. Hundreds of times in the past seven years people have said to me: "You are so brave to tell. I'm afraid to tell my employer that I have a mental illness." And they are right to be afraid. Employees are fired, passed over, and marginalized at work when they disclose. And I wonder. What if we were talking about diabetes or asthma or cancer? Does it require bravery to tell our employers about these illnesses? Are these people also fired, passed over, or marginalized at work?
>
> I don't believe that systemic change in [the workplace] will happen until we who have this so-called invisible disability are seen. We don't have to share details, we just have to be seen. Six million of us—your family, friends, co-workers and neighbours. I wonder what would happen if we who are well and are secure in our employment come out en masse. At a staff meeting, board meeting, team meeting maybe we could simply say, without fanfare or production, "I would like to celebrate Mental Health Week by identifying as one of the six million [of my fellows] who will have a mental illness in their lifetime. I have a mental illness." Essentially with these words we are saying: I belong to that group AND I belong to you.

or sugar. In case you're wondering: yes, it was humiliating. But that was the least of my worries at the time.)

Ask neighbors or friends to walk the dog, pick up those tampons you needed yesterday, or chauffeur your other kids to their after-school commitments. If you're too broke to pay them or too exhausted to reciprocate in kind, explain the situation in whatever way feels comfortable to you. Offer them an IOU for some *manageable* favor in return (which you can delegate to a willing family member, if necessary).

- *When you just can't find an alternative route . . .*
  - *Let it go!* Defer, cancel, improvise. Come what may, accept that you did everything you could. Best advice I never listened to—until recently. It takes practice, but if you're a mental health parent you're up to pretty much any challenge!

3. *When you do make it out, what tactics can help you keep on* task, *not* off kilter?

- *Set up for success:*
  - Explain exactly what's about to come—as simply and matter-of-factly as possible.

    Hanna, here's what we're going to do this morning:

    First—we have to go to the bank. I need you to come in with me and wait patiently till I finish up. There'll be chairs there and you can bring a book.

    Second—after the bank, we'll head to the drugstore. I have to buy three necessary things and there's no money for extras, so it's going to be quick!

    Third—after the drugstore, we'll go straight home so you can get back to watching TV.

    Strategies like this sometimes worked like a charm for my kids, especially when they were younger. Other times, they didn't work at all. Either way, it can't hurt to draw for your child a mental (or pictorial, or written) itinerary before you go out. As you already know, emotionally dysregulated kids tend to struggle with transitions.
  - Incentivize and reward emotional stability (but *don't* punish dysregulated behavior when she can't help it—which is pretty much always, as psychiatric disorder is never a choice). Tell her if she keeps her cool through her dental appointment, you can celebrate with a visit to that doughnut shop across the street afterward. If she can't totally

keep it together in the dental chair, but between you and any out-of-the-box thinkers on staff, the appointment is concluded with no "collateral damage" (e.g., injuries to clinicians or major disturbance of other patients), get her a doughnut. In return, ask her to process what happened—if not now, then later. If she self-regulates immediately after you leave the office, that's even better—give her a high five! Offer her as many opportunities for success as possible . . . provided your definition of "success" makes sense—for her and you.

- *Break out the head phones/earbuds.* Encourage your kid(s) to listen to music, an audiobook, or a favorite podcast while idling in the therapist's waiting room or cruising the aisles of your local supermarket. You might even make it nonnegotiable, with the promise of a reward on the other end. ("Joe, we're short on time. I'd appreciate your listening to your book while we shop, so I can just grab what we need, and we can get in and out of here fast, without distraction. Then, we'll have time for a latte and a muffin.")

  While my example here seems more appropriate for younger kids, you can successfully use this tactic with teens too. Adolescents with or without emotional disorders indulge in escape-through-earbuds all the time. On those occasions they have to accompany you while you do your thing, they'll be happy to zone out on music while pretending they don't know you.

- *Let a fluffy therapist take over some of the hard stuff for you.* The previous chapter talked about the benefits of a family pet for regulating life at home—*if* your living situation (and personal inclinations) are animal friendly. Furry, four-legged "therapists" can bring the whole family's blood pressure down, and be particularly healing for your emotionally disordered kid. A specially trained therapy animal (or a naturally chill pet) may help get you and/or your kid out the door, and enable everyone to keep calm and carry on! Whether you're headed to school, the store, the barbershop, or to take the PSATs, allow your kid (and yourself) to spend ten minutes beforehand in furry or purry embrace. If your pet is comfortable in the car, and can wait *safely and happily* behind while you do what you have to do, take her with you— portable comfort! For a dysregulated kid, snuggling with a pet in the car can be consoling, regulating, even empowering. Just make sure your fluffy therapist has a calm, sociable personality and enjoys doing his job!

TIP: Do the right thing and be sure you have the resources to care for another dependent family member *before* you start Googling "support dog" or "helper monkey." And—you knew this was coming, didn't you?—tap into your parent networks for ideas on introducing a pet into an often-challenging atmosphere.

- *Pare down your to-do list.* Remember that moment in *The Wizard of Oz* when Dorothy notices she's not in Kansas anymore? Right. So, when you tell yourself you're going to "run out" and tackle the eight errands on your list tomorrow, have yourself a Dorothy moment and cross off five of them before you even start. You are not living the life you used to live. This is a lesson my rheumatologist taught me, after I developed an autoimmune disease from ten years straight of living in Mom-Bot mode. It's a keeper. You just have to wrap your head around the fact that what you think you *ought* to accomplish is irrelevant. What's possible in the present is limited by circumstances beyond your control. Think of your new reality as a mere fact, not a moral or constitutional flaw. Anyway, even the superyou wouldn't really have gotten all that stuff done in a single morning—right?

Escape Plan Nitty-Gritties

It goes without saying that you've been practicing the art of nimble adaptation to an environment—and kid—in constant flux, because you are a mental health parent, and frankly, it's adapt, or . . . let's not even go there.

If you've read up to this point, you know that some outings/escapes can be rerouted, if not canceled or postponed. Whether you take time off or work from home, shop online, recruit friends to take the canary to the vet, or resign yourself to cleaning dog poop off the rug—delayed or detoured leave-takings don't have to be a catastrophe.

And you also know that you can create an itinerary, in written, pictorial, or spoken form, for a kid who needs the comfort of a structured plan. You can use distractions, incentives and rewards (some might call them "bribes"), or even a furry "therapist" to help you get yourselves to the places you need to be. You will use these strategies again and again, tweaking them as necessary, replacing them with better ones as your understanding of your child evolves.

This is how you will (mostly) get out the door and on your way. But what about when you reach your destination?

As fate would have it, *stuff happens* once you're in public places. Between the moment you enter the supermarket and the moment you return to your car, five or ten perceived (or actual) provocations could trip your kid's emotional breakers.

That's where the nitty-gritties of your escape plans—the *specific* measures you take to manage the unexpected (and unwelcome) hits *in real time*—come in.

You know too well what dangers lurk in everyday places: a stranger's glower, a misinterpreted comment, an intentional or accidental jostle. Too many people in one place, too few in another. Nonspecific panic that rises out of nowhere. All those unsatisfied desires a kid with an eternal ache in her heart faces everywhere, every day—because the world is filled with things, material and emotional, she wants but can't have.

The subtlest jab can puncture bone deep into a kid whose protective layers are thin to nonexistent. That's why the world can be such a treacherous place for mental health families, and one of many reasons why we need working strategies to get us out there and back in one piece.

We're Out, It's Happening. What Do I Do Now?
(Sample On-the-Go Responses to Some Typical Public Meltdowns)

- *Problem:* Your child reacts explosively to your question or touch in a confined space—a train platform, perhaps, or a farmers' market—and bystanders are clearly uncomfortable. Or maybe your young adult is experiencing auditory hallucinations, triggered by a new medication. The folks you encounter in the elevators and hallways of University Hospital, en route to the psychiatric clinic, are understandably unsettled—even frightened. In either case, you want to explain the situation discreetly, without humiliating or provoking your kid.
- *Solution:* Carry a stack of double-sided "public education/information cards" with you at all times, and hand them out to anyone who could use a bit of education—or, on the flip side, deserves a thank-you. (Creds to Will's mom, Caroline, for this genius idea. You can get reacquainted with Caroline and Will in chapter 1.)

[front] *The young person I am with has a mental health disorder known as [your child's diagnosis]. Sometimes this causes him to act in ways that might seem unfamiliar or scary. Please know that he can't help it, and that we are trying our best to manage his illness. We appreciate your keeping our feelings in mind before you criticize or judge. For more information, please go to www .[organization of choice].com. Thank you for reading this!*

[back] *My child and I would like to thank you from the bottom of our hearts for your compassion today. She has a mental health disorder known as [your child's diagnosis]. Sometimes this causes her to act in ways that might seem unfamiliar or scary. Your thoughtfulness and understanding mean a lot to us. www.[organization of choice].com*

- *Problem:* Blunt, cruel, or abusive comments from strangers.
- *Solutions (presuming you don't have your "information cards" on you—or are too pissed off to use them):*
  - Go on, imagine briefly that punch in the nose. Then remind yourself you are not *ever* allowed to actually punch a nose—or let on to your kid you wish you could. (True story: I once had to suppress an urge to push a third grader off his bike. He whizzed past us and insulted my kid as we walked to school. Poised to sprint after him, I thought, *I can totally take that squirt!* Fortunately for everyone, I came to my senses. And if I hadn't, I'm a very slow runner, so that's good.)
  - Practice the fine art of sarcasm—either in your sweetest revenge fantasies, or in real life. You have my permission. Really. *Why, yes, we ARE doing this just to annoy you.*
  - Simply inform the offender that your child has a diagnosis of whatever, and that comments of this kind are ignorant and extremely hurtful. (This is most appropriate spoken matter-of-factly, in a low voice—preferably out of your kid's and any bystanders' earshot.)
  - Hug your kid if she'll let you, tell her audibly that bullies come in all ages, shapes, and sizes, and that people who are mean to others feel bad about themselves. Then remind her that you love her—even when she's having a tough time.

- ○ Cry—ideally, after you get home and have some privacy. But this one's probably a last resort, or an add-on to one of the others.
- *Problem:* Well-meaning but unwelcome advice, from strangers, acquaintances, and/or relatives.
- *Solution:* Smile brightly and say something like, "Appreciate it, we're good. It's all under control." Then, just carry on. If they persist, tell them you'll be in touch when you need some expert advice. Sometimes a little snark can be therapeutic—just make sure you don't cross any lines or model behavior you'd be mortified to see your kid picking up.
- *Problem:* Your child is harassed, excluded, or even expelled from public places. (Another true story: there is a hair salon in Boston that once firmly and loudly invited us to never, ever return after four-year-old Benjy had a panic attack in the hands of one of their stylists. Thirteen years later, my skin still crawls when I'm within a few blocks of that place.)
- *Solutions:*
  - ○ Why the heck are you going to places with words like "Salon" or "Bistro" in their names, anyway? *Kids of all stripes* are why child-friendly haircut franchises, or your laid-back local family diner, exist. Ask your parent networks—local Facebook groups, fellow school parents, some random mom on the playground—for suggestions. Sometimes there's a "comb doctor" (as my daughter used to call hairstylists) who just *gets* our kids, or the perfect, humble breakfast place, right in your neighborhood. You just never noticed.
  - ○ Sigh deeply and modify your expectations of the human race. Many folks can't intuit interior trauma, or understand some behaviors as signals of emotional disorder. Hey, people are only human, you know? But you may have an opportunity to educate them, *if* you feel up to the task. For example, you could . . .
    - Explain briefly and calmly that what just happened was not a choice
    - Suggest they try putting themselves in your shoes
    - Whip out your information cards and pass them around
    - Remind the proprietor (and anyone else who needs to know) that there's a civil rights law called the ADA (Americans with Disabilities Act). And that if they kick you out

because your kid has a mental health disorder, they're violating it. I'm guessing that's all you'll need to say. If the problem persists, you can file a civil rights complaint against the establishment.[2]

The Evil Eye: Be Aware, Be Prepared

We've all been pinned by it—the glare from that officious person in the supermarket, who knows better than we do how to deal with our kids, even if our kids are just kids having a bad day. Most parents have had at least one dressing-down by some know-it-all in the produce aisle who thinks their parenting skills suck.

For mental health parents, these painful encounters are plentiful. They're scary. The kind of event that makes parents pray the earth will yawn beneath them and swallow them whole. Or better yet, swallow the know-it-all.

That's just life with an emotionally dysregulated kid. Managing a thirteen-year-old's aggressive outburst while browsing the sporting goods store (which you *knew* was a lousy idea in the first place) is brutal stuff. Also, it's everyday stuff that even parents with children who do not have a diagnosis occasionally face.

It helps to be mentally prepared for what folks may be thinking when they encounter you and your kid riding out a psychiatric storm—if only so you can reassure yourself that it's *them*, not *you*, who lacks understanding of the situation. Here are a few of the common assumptions you will meet in public—often unspoken but still painful—if you haven't already:

OH, THE THINGS THEY'RE THINKING!

1. What a crappy parent—obviously wouldn't know a limit if it smacked her on the butt.
2. *Typical.* Mom's on the phone while kid's wreaking havoc in public. Probably setting up a pedicure for tomorrow.
3. This child clearly needs help. Why haven't his parents done something about his behavioral issues?
4. *Your daughter* is disrupting all the other kids' playtime. Maybe she doesn't belong at this playground. . . .

Why does it help to know misconceptions like these are out there, and how to decode the words and gestures that convey them? Because, by speaking out in response, parents like us can help foster the change our families need. Let the ones who make you feel unwanted and incompetent know what's really going on—and how it feels to be in your shoes!

Not that it's easy. Too many times, I could not find the voice to speak truth to ignorance when I was desperately dialing my child's therapist on my cell phone (or texting an SOS to my husband) and simultaneously triaging a mental health crisis in public. Lots of times you won't find yours, either. It's triumph enough to simply keep yourself from keeling over with exhaustion.

Still, someday there may come a moment of empowerment, when you remember you have a voice and how to use it. Best then to know what to say, and how to say it.

Reader, let's make a pact to speak truth to ignorance, and to encourage understanding in people who haven't yet figured us out. Not necessarily now, maybe not tomorrow. *Just sometime, when we can.*

PARENT STORY: "SHE COULDN'T 'READ' THE OUTSIDE WORLD": RENA AND JACOB'S STORY

Rena and Jacob are parents to fourteen-year-old Jessie and eight-year-old Adam. I can see fatigue, worry, and sadness etched in their faces—especially Rena's, as she's most often been fighting on the front line while Jacob has (tried) to earn enough to cover the family's mental health care and related expenses.

According to Rena, from Jessie's earliest days her anxiety and other, undiagnosed psychiatric disorders made being out in public difficult. As first-time parents, Rena and Jacob had no idea what was going on . . . only noticing that their much-loved little girl was "different" than her peers. That meant the whole family was often misunderstood, and felt disliked and unwelcomed when they ventured out into the world.

Rena: When Jessie was in preschool one of her teachers took me aside and said, "I think she has bipolar disorder." I mean, who the hell says a thing like that to a parent? I guess what she was trying to say was, *Your daughter is unable to function in the social universe of this classroom.* I hated her for that, but of course, it was basically true. Jessie did not play well except in twos. She'd latch onto another kid so fiercely, and then when a third tried to enter into whatever they were doing, Jess would totally erupt and say, "You get away! You can't play here!" We'd see that too, on the playground. Jacob or I would always try to gently intervene—"No, honey, this game is for *all* the children, this is how we play!"—but she was so intense, and so angry, it never worked. The stress of managing these interactions was so, just unbelievable, you cannot imagine. Because it felt like everyone in the outside world hated us.

Jacob: We were new parents, you know? We didn't know what this experience was "supposed" to be like, but it's painfully obvious when *your* kid is not like all the other kids. The other parents don't hesitate to let you know it, either.

Rena: So eventually we realized that she was just *so* anxious. Like, that intense jealousy on the playground, or what people saw as hostility and aggression, was just Jessie being scared to death out there. Of losing a connection to another kid? Of being out in the world and not doing it right?

Jacob: She did end up with all those diagnoses, too. Bipolar, anxiety, autism spectrum.

Rena: Yeah. And remember all those babysitters who quit? No one could handle her! Once she was out in the park with a sitter, and there was a youth soccer game going on, and Jess broke away from this girl and ran *right across the soccer field* in the middle of the game. She was old enough at that time to know. . . .

Jacob: What was she, eight or nine? Seven?

Rena: Right. And they had to *stop the game* while that sitter tried to corral her, and Jessie was laughing and laughing. . . . Oh my God. So, there was really no keeping a sitter for more than one or two gigs. I think the worst of it was the everlasting feeling we were sinking. And knowing that Jessie's behaviors were signals of pain.

Jacob: This kind of parenting does not come naturally. The stress is beyond belief. And just because you finally have a diagnosis, and she's under treatment, in therapy, on psych meds, doesn't mean it gets magically better.

Rena: Does it ever?

Jacob: Man, I hope so.

Rena: That awful social anxiety is ongoing—for our whole family. Because you never know what's going to happen next, except most likely you and your kid are going to get that *look*. The mean and mad look.

Jacob: She *is* doing better than she was, though. Small increments.

Rena: Yup. Baby steps.

Read more about Rena, Jacob, and family in chapter 5.

WHEN YOU WANT OR NEED TO
STEP OUT ON YOUR OWN . . .

In the early to middle years of my own mental health parenting, my ability and desire to take care of myself diminished. I had my places to go, all of them dictated and circumscribed by the demands of my child's (and eventually, my own) illness. Medical offices, hospitals, pharmacies, supermarkets, the homes of family and friends (but only if they were close by, or Lars could go with me). The byways I *did* travel I learned by heart, driving on autopilot, always as alert to the internal doings of the boy behind or beside me as I was to the road. When Saskia was with us, there were two young inner lives to be monitored—and one less-valued one on the periphery (mine), to be repressed.

There were no places I could go for pleasure—not because someone told me no, but because I lost the emotional ability to move freely about in the world; to sever, even temporarily, the cords that bound my family together. Fear had colonized me. Every conscious breath, glance, taste, or touch, reminded me that the world was dangerous, and only my extreme attention could save not just my boy, but Lars and Saskia too—the three people in this world I loved most.

This was a crappy way to live. Unfortunately, it was all I knew, the only way I could figure out to put one foot in front of the other and keep crawling forward. I wish I'd discovered a better way. *That* way drained the life and health right out of me.

Because I approached managing mental illness so reactively, I eventually saw firsthand how destructive a force it can be, for a patient, a caregiver, and an entire family. The good news is that I learned from the experience—which is the reason I wrote this book, and stay actively involved in my own parent networks. This is how I continue to pay it forward as I keep learning new things. And in turn, I can benefit from my fellows-in-adversity when I need their wisdom and support.

On that note, here are some suggestions for breaking through the limits of fear, and recovering the inner life you may have lost:

1. Make a list of things you might like to do alone, with family or friends, or with people you don't know.
2. Tape your list in a place where you'll easily see it—the fridge door comes to mind—or next to the notes of encouragement you may have posted for yourself after reading chapter 1 ("Steps You Can Take Right Now"). Read the list regularly, even if it takes you

weeks or more to find an opening and try something out. Every time you contemplate doing some activity on your list but don't make it, congratulate yourself for trying. Tomorrow's another day, and baby steps are still steps.

3. Consider asking family or friends for help in meeting your goal of getting out and taking care of you. Just make sure they understand that *this is a judgment-free zone.* They're not allowed to give you grief if you can't quite get there yet.

   - For birthday/holiday gifts, tell people who ask that a gift card to your favorite coffeehouse would be a great way to get you out of the house—alone or with company. People in my life have more than once surprised me with gift cards for indulgences like coffee shops and massage—right in my email inbox. My joy was indescribable—and these gestures showed me I was worth caring for. Don't wait for others to take the lead, though: buy the Starbucks card yourself, and use it! (Websites like Groupon.com and LivingSocial.com can help reduce the sting by as much as 50 percent.)

   - If finances are tight (and whose aren't, these days?) your loved ones can still help you get out of your shrinking, and often toxic, comfort zone when your kid is safe/cared for at present and you can get out. My mom used to call me every day when I was at my lowest point, to nudge me gently into getting out. Ben had entered a residential school at just thirteen. I was broken by the loss of him, and bewildered by what seemed a heavy idleness in my life, but was actually the beginning of a new, healing phase. Even though I was bodily and emotionally wrecked, she encouraged me to take tiny steps outward. "Could you take a walk around the block? Why don't you, Lars, Saskia go out to eat tonight? You won't betray Benjy by trying to move beyond the pain." My mom's a smart woman. She knew I had to learn, just like we hoped our Ben would finally be learning, how to press on and live.

4. Change your perspective!

   - Take a walk (or drive) in a new neighborhood. Observe everything, using all your senses. Breathe. It all sounds so basic, so obvious. I know. But after you finish thinking, *For this I needed a book?* ask yourself this question: *Do I actually do it?* (If you do, then my apologies for stating the useless and obvious. If you don't, take this as a gentle reminder—and remind yourself again tomorrow.) When you allow yourself a change of scenery and sensory perception, it helps you feel alive again.

- Do the above, but bring a friend. Or a dog. Or both! If you have your own dog(s) but have been delegating walks to your partner or kids or paid dog-walker, get back to it. Here's an equation even non–mathy types, like me, can understand: walking + fresh air + wagging tails = natural mood lifter. When I developed my autoimmune disease on top of my existing anxiety, depression, and chronic pain, I cheated on the dog-walking if I couldn't rope anyone else into doing it for me. Why did the damn dog need to go out on winter nights, anyway? I'd take him, but it was like, "Get busy!" and as soon as he got busy, "Hey—wanna cookie? Let's go home!" which meant those walks were over in a New York minute, all business and no pleasure. When I made the decision to rediscover the pleasure in our walks—one of my better life decisions—there it was, all this calm and stillness and satisfaction, waiting for me.

- Replace "cat" and "dog" (but not "human friend"—never!) with the animal of your choice, and find a way to interact. Changes of scenery can be an indoor phenomenon too, you know. Volunteer at a shelter. Find families in town who could use a pet sitter when they go out of town, and dote on their critters. If you do, you'll enrich more than one life!

- If you're not an animal-obsessive like me, no worries! There are other means to the same end. It may sound corny, but just listen to your body, brain, and heart, then figure out how to nourish them. Whether it's good food, exercise, music, dancing, reading, knitting, gardening, sleep, sex, recultivating neglected friendships, or what have you, value yourself enough to do it for *you*. Start small and work your way to big(ger). *Focusing on you does* not *equal neglecting your family.* On the contrary—you're tending to the parts of you that need to stay strong for them.

OUR STORY: SNAPSHOTS #5–#8

#5.   The boundaries of my world begin to contract, as going out with two challenging kids and one me gets harder and harder. The more stressful life becomes, the more time Lars seems to spend at work. Benjy's triggers are everywhere: a car or a room entered first by someone other than he; a breeze, gusty or feathery, across his skin; a stranger's glance or smile, which can only mean one thing to Ben—mockery.

As time passes and Ben's emotional breakdowns increase in number and intensity, I travel the same path over and over again, usually with him, sometimes with Saskia, occasionally with both. From school to my ill-fated work to school again to doctors' offices to hospitals to home to therapy to the supermarket, and occasionally to my brother's house ten miles down the highway. I can make these trips alone, but rarely have the opportunity. After a while I'm no longer sure I can carry the weight of that aloneness in my car, and opt out of traveling within or beyond my new perimeter unless I have someone with me.

#6.   I have to choose between attending Saskia's voice recitals and band concerts and staying home with Ben, whose claustrophobic, agoraphobic tendencies make concerts and recitals impossible for him. Sometimes Lars stays home and I go. Sometimes no one goes to Saskia's performances except the parents of her friends and a lot of strangers. I feel a deadly pull from opposite directions. If I weren't petrified of becoming an addict and neglecting my kids, I'd dig out a couple of Ativan and wash them down with a tumbler of Three-Buck Chuck. Instead, I think about my daughter, performing to an audience without her family, and imagine my son, left behind while I watch his sister's performance, and I will myself into a frozen state. I can take care of Ben and miss Saskia's performance while self-anesthetized, and it will kind of turn out all right.

#7.   I try to attend an academic conference for the first time since I had kids. I'm giving a talk on Charles Dickens's novel *Hard Times*. It should be a breeze, because before motherhood and maladies of the psyche took over my life, I was a Dickens scholar—and besides, this is a Mickey Mouse conference. I've done far bigger and better than *this* dumb event.

I leave Lars and the kids at home and set off for a whole long day, driving to the conference with the chair of my department. (I teach at a college where I'm a lowly adjunct professor, one of the day laborers of academia.) I could have driven myself, but she invited me along for the ride. Good thing too, as I no longer drive outside of my newly redrawn district—and also, because you never know what good things can happen when you rub shoulders with the highly placed and well connected.

Nothing good happens. I obsessively check my phone for messages all day and into the evening, in case Ben flays himself while Lars watches baseball, or Saskia tries cooking something on the stove and sets her clothes on fire. When I give my talk, I continually misspeak the name of a very well-known Dickens character. Of course, some jerk uses the Q&A to point that out. Thank you very much!

As soon as my session ends, I flip open my dumb-phone and tap in my voice mail passcode again. It's like a tic. I've probably already lost my job, anyway, between the unforced errors in my own talk and my obvious dysfunction during the conference keynote speech, early in the day—a very good one, in fact, and on the subject of *character names in Dickens*, funnily enough. When I flipped my phone and started dialing, about two minutes into that talk, my department chair looked at me like she wanted to strangle me.

#8.   A friend, who teaches master's students in special education at a university in Boston, invites me to attend a graduate seminar taught by her colleague and offer up the perspective of disability parent. This is the best idea I've heard from an educator since becoming a disability parent. Because no special educator, no special education administrator, gets what living this life, 24/7, is like—unless they're doing it themselves. Which probably doesn't happen very often.

"Yes!" I say, with a tingling sense that I *might* be about to start changing the world, one tiny change at a time.

A week before the scheduled class, the tingling turns into a slow, crawling burn. I am scared out of my wits. That university is in south Boston, *way* out of my zone. Plus, who's going to watch the kids? Oh yeah, Lars. I love Lars. Lars loves the kids. But even on a good day, Lars and Ben, and Lars and Saskia, and Saskia and Ben are oil and water. Also, it has happened, once or twice, that Lars forgot Benjy is on psych meds, or decided those meds are only a suggestion. And I would not put it past him to take the two kids out without bug spray, even though it's summer and a bad year for mosquito-borne illnesses in Massachusetts.

I'm not saying he's not a keeper, Lars. He's just not *me*.

Ben has been trying to make it through a week of Suzuki violin "camp." The week goes from *meh* to a *code red*. This class is scheduled for Friday, the last day of violin camp. At 10 a.m. I get the first call. "I think you might probably want to pick him up, if that's OK with you," the poor girl at the front desk whispers into the phone. I'm deep in the last-minute prep for my classroom gig, trying to make my brain work faster.

"Can you keep him another hour, do you think?"

After a pause, she whispers, "We'll try."

Of course, I'm in my car before a quarter hour passes. How can I concentrate on this damned class when Ben is breaking? I never make it to south Boston. And I never change the world with my heartbreaking testimony in front of a bunch of MA candidates in special education. What a damned relief! I was never going to drive down there, park on some unfamiliar street with a forgettable name like "A Street," find the right classroom in the right building, and talk about our lives, anyway. I haven't even figured out yet how you live like this and brush your teeth on a daily basis. Have I?

Links to Escape Resources

IN CASE A CHILD'S ILLNESS PULLS YOU
AWAY FROM THE WORKPLACE . . .

- The Family and Medical Leave Act: https://www.dol.gov/whd/fmla/
- Donna Hardaker, consultant on managing mental illness and wellness in the workplace: http://donnahardaker.com/

FOR WHEN YOU WANT SOME FOUR-LEGGED HELP . . .

Service animals are lifesavers for some folks, but they're not for everyone. First, you have to qualify as requiring one—and usually that means you have a physical impairment that prevents completion of activities of daily living (ADLs). Second, the cost can be staggering, although many organizations will help with that.

Kids with psychiatric challenges, unless they also have severe physical impairments, are more likely to benefit from therapeutic or emotional assistance animals. These tend to be dogs, and are sometimes used in visits with their owners to nursing homes, schools, and other institutions where people would benefit from their presence. In our home we have a dog, who would fail the chill test in two seconds flat, and a bunny, who is our chiller in chief. Both adopted from local shelters, although there's more than one path to this particular nirvana.

Before you take any steps, familiarize yourself with regulations, definitions, and sources of therapeutic pets here:

- https://www.ada.gov/regs2010/service_animal_qa.html
- https://www.nsarco.com/therapy-animal-info.htmlwww.ASPCA.org

Wanna walk dogs, for fun and profit?

- www.Rover.com
- www.Care.com

FOR WHEN YOU'RE READY TO HAVE YOUR "PUBLIC EDUCATION" CARDS PRINTED UP . . .

- www.vistaprint.com
- www.staples.com

Or if you're up to the challenge, just DIY it with a printer and some cardstock!

OPEN MIC: KIDS SPEAK OUT!

Emily F., Age Twenty-Six, Pennsylvania

I was one of those kids who was always on the sidelines, because I was different. Because I am on the autism spectrum, and I have bipolar disorder and OCD and some learning differences, I generally have to work harder at life than "typical" people do. I have a high IQ, but learning in school was challenging, until my parents found the right school for me. I've always struggled with social situations and reading body language, stuff like that. I'm lucky that my parents understood me and worked tirelessly on my behalf. Not every kid has parents who can do that. My story could have been tragic, but honestly, I think I'm pretty successful, in spite of everything.

If I were to advise parents of kids with significant challenges, I would say, "Never say never." And to the kids? "You are going to keep surprising yourself!"

I used to secretly think, *I'll never make it through middle school!* And then I did. *I'll never graduate high school and go to college!* But I did. I thought I couldn't possibly hold down a full-time job. And you know what? Just recently I was promoted from part-time to full-time magic shop clerk and dragon slayer! I wear a costume and help little kids find and slay "dragons." I know, right? I don't make a lot of money, but I'm valued at work, I live independently (with my partner of seven years!), and I make a difference in some kids' lives. I'm happy with that.

My personal success probably has a lot to do with how I've learned to manage my mental health issues in various settings, including at school and work. My parents are amazing; they really helped me with managing my own challenges and advocating for myself.

The best lessons my parents taught me?

1. To know, value, and trust myself
2. To be open to all possibilities
3. To be willing to try, and fail, and try again
4. To self-advocate, and believe I could be a partner in my own treatment and education plans
5. To understand my limits, when to be open to new experiences, and when to step back
6. To always prepare in advance. Preview new places before I go; find out all the details of social events in advance, so I can make a reasonable exit plan if I need one.
7. To be proud and be honest. Sometimes it's important to disclose your issues to others, so they can understand you, and hopefully accept you as you are.

THE TAKEAWAY

- Get out and live your life! The whole family will benefit from active involvement in the world outside your walls. Just know when the better choice is to hunker down and wait for the inner turmoil to pass.
- Alternative routes to a fully functional life abound. Find them, create them, remake them—and *use them when you need to*!
- Keep in mind that *your* "normal" is just that. It's not the status quo of your siblings or neighbors or anything you read in the mainstream parenting books or watch on TV. It may not always be pretty, but it's yours. If you can somehow learn to cherish your everyday life *as it is*—like you do with the people you love—you'll probably be happier and healthier. But hey—I know, I just asked you to climb Mount Rushmore naked, at the height of tourist season. I'll forgive you if it takes a lot of preparation before you can do it!
- Your "escape plans" are the tools that will make every point above possible. They take time and resilience to develop. They require a lot of trial and error (and error, and error) because there's no blueprint—every single one of them is specific to you, your kid, and the moment. Still: *don't give up!* Escape plans work.

4

WHEN SCHOOL MAKES
YOUR KID SICK(ER)

Almost every day I cross paths with parents whose kids have trouble at school—a school *aversion*, severe enough that it affects the whole family.

These are often quick encounters. Yet almost always, between the breezy greeting and the sympathetic farewell, language like "anxiety," "depression," and "*I don't know what to do!*" gets strewn about. Not to mention the mutual head shakes, followed by, "Well, you'll/we'll get through it—*somehow.*"

For a sizable number of kids, from preschool through high school, education is a soul-sucking, learning-deficient affair. This statistic, also cited in chapter 1, is really no surprise: one in five schoolchildren—or five out of the twenty-five kids in a typical public school classroom—have, have had, or will have a disabling mental health disorder.[1] Think about it.

THE SCHOOL / MENTAL HEALTH CONNECTION

You might wonder if school plays a significant role in what seems to be an epidemic of childhood mental health disorders. Well, you *should* be wondering—first, because there's a lot of factual evidence to support that concern, and second, because it just makes no sense that school is hurting so many of our kids.

School's not meant to suck the spirit out of our children—at least in theory.

In practice, though, students with disabilities (including, but not limited to, kids with significant psychiatric involvement) slip through the cracks every hour of every day. It's a big problem. If only we, readers, could put our heads together and solve it! Even the folks who make their careers at solving problems in education haven't been able to do it. No surprise there, given that education is not just about educating, but also about politics and ideology, the marketplace, training, access to resources, and the goodwill of a whole lot of people with power and their own agendas.

KIDS WITH DISABILITIES ARE ENTITLED TO A FREE AND APPROPRIATE PUBLIC EDUCATION (A "FAPE"). SO, WHY WORRY? ACTIVIST AND ADVOCATE CYNTHIA MOORE EXPLAINS WHY.

We all know that the field of education attracts people with big hearts and a passion for improving children's lives. But here's something that might surprise you: no matter how well intentioned the people, money drives every decision a school district makes about a child with special needs. Sometimes, these include decisions that result in suffering for students and their families.

Why? Because American public education mirrors American society—it's based on capitalism rather than humanism. The legal protections granted to students with disabilities *persistently fail* due to the system's design.[2] There are no immediate, automatic consequences when a school district violates a student's educational rights. For all intents and purposes, then, success is defined in relation to the maintenance or reduction of the school district's budget.

In other words, the democratic principles underlying the Individuals with Disabilities Education Act (IDEA)[3] can only be fulfilled by divorcing educational decisions about a student from decision-makers who are beholden to a budget.

The model we have now rewards the salesperson (school district) for selling a product (a "not-so-individualized" education plan) they know won't work, to a client (student/family) who needs a different, more customized solution—all in the interest of cost control. Tell me: In what other line of business would that model of operation be sustainable? In the commercial realm, where consumers are at least nominally protected, the widespread dishonest dealing we see in the American special education system would be considered fraudulent.

Protection of disability rights in education is an ongoing battle. Given the limitations of the system we've got, the best outcomes for kids are linked to active, informed, parent involvement and vigorous advocacy.[4]

FIVE THINGS I WISH I KNEW FROM THE BEGINNING

1. If your kid is struggling with mental health issues at home, he or she is bound to be struggling at school—even if you're not aware of it.
2. Even the "best" schools are often ill equipped to support students with psychiatric (and other) challenges. The worst of them are as bad as prisons . . . and they can be adept at hiding it.
3. Mental illnesses are disabilities, and *do* impact a student's education. If your kid is in public school, request a special education evaluation, ASAP—and make sure to pursue evaluations conducted by professionals independent from your school district as well.
4. As with every other aspect of mental health parenting, grasping the ins and outs of your child's profile and educational rights can be mind-blowingly hard. Forgive yourself if it takes time to figure things out—you're in good company. If you can afford it, hire a (good) special education advocate to help you through the process. Above all, keep dishing out heaps of love and support—in that special way only you can do for your child.
5. There is no shame in bailing out of a school that's sinking your kid. Reach out to your parent networks for suggestions and support as you work through the situation. While their laypersons' input is no substitute for professional advice from a qualified education advocate, they can definitely help you get started on your plan B (or C, or D . . .).

SCHOOL IS NOT YOUR KID'S JOB
(AT LEAST, NOT IN THE WAY YOU THOUGHT IT WAS)

When Saskia and Ben were little, I tried to sell them on the notion that school was their job. As in, "I know, Monday is the worst, but see how Mom and Dad go to work anyway? School is just your office. And when you get there and get busy, it's not so bad after all."

I have probably committed more offenses against the Gospel of Good Parenting than you can count on all your fingers and toes, plus a few extra! And the old "School is your job, so you have to go even if you hate it" rule might be among my worst insults to my own children's intelligence and well-being.

Sure, kids in America do have to go to school—and they're lucky to have the chance. The thing is, when Lars or I have had an unbearable, soul-crushing, stomach-churning job, we have either quit (me) or hung on by the skin of our teeth while doggedly looking for another one (Lars). Which means the command to just suck it up because it's a job is an attitude we have modeled most of the time—but not when things at work reach crisis proportion.

For example, when the boss is a bully. Or the company is unethical. Or we are being horribly, terribly exploited. Or, when we (OK, *I*) kind of oversold our skills in the interview, and suddenly realized "we" could *not* do that job. School can be exactly like that. School is work's "mini-me." But your kid is not you, and the situations aren't parallel.

A child—especially, but not exclusively, a kid with a disability—can feel as wretched, as unable to succeed, and as demoralized in school as an adult can at work. (Oddly enough, I *was* that demoralized kid in school, so I have no clue why it took me so long to figure this out regarding my own children!) Increase the misery if the child has a significant mental health problem, which by definition, makes coping all the harder.

In other words: your child deserves at least the chance of an escape—a better option for her—when the "job" she works is slowly draining her spirit.

Whether the issue is bullying, a high-stress environment, sensory overload, or a one-size-fits-all teaching model, some schools will *never be a good fit for your kid*, no matter how hard you and others try to make it so. When your child is emotionally disordered, a bad fit can have a devastating outcome.

Look Out for Signs Your Kid Is "School-Sick"
(or School Is Sick of Your Kid)

Yep, "school-sick" is a nonclinical, nonteacherly term, made up by me. Still, it'll hit a nerve for many, many people who have a stake in the education of children. Ouch.

If you're reading this book, I'm guessing you already know quite a few things about "school-sickness" and the strain it can place on a child and family. You may be one of the legion of parents who are all too familiar with:

- Daily phone calls from school insisting you come get your kid and take him home. (Unspoken truth: the school cannot safely or effectively educate him.)
- Lack of communication from school about issues directly involving your child, such as revoked privileges or other punitive measures; injuries inflicted by self, peers, or staff; and similar troubling incidents. (Unspoken truth: it's easier for the school to avoid costly responsibility/bad publicity if they don't tell Mom or Dad.)
- "Loss" of your child or teen for a period of time after she bolted in a rage or panic, and no one noticed for several minutes. You only find out about it when another parent emails you to confirm the veracity of the rumor. (Unspoken truth: see truths 1 and 2, above.)
- Teachers and aides who perceive your kid as "lazy," "bad," or otherwise morally broken—and are more than happy to share their assessment with the classroom at large. (Unspoken truth: qualified classroom help is expensive! And with twenty-eight students and a boatload of paperwork to manage, you think the teacher is going to take time to "read the manual" that comes with kids like yours?)
- Bubbly assurances from teachers that *he's doing just great!* Which sounds fishy, because he comes home every day worse for the wear—like, with holes gnawed through his shirt and half-moon lacerations on his cheeks, the very size and shape of his own ragged fingernails. (Unspoken truth: good, sweet, and overwhelmed teacher thinks, *Ohmygod this* kid! *He's not okay, he's not okay! But it's probably just me. I'm sure he's doing* great, *deep down inside . . . maybe those are old chew holes. Anyway, he's doing* awesome *and I just love him!* You know you love her back, but still . . .)
- Overall good-faith efforts to educate your child with compassion . . . but he can't get out of his fetal position long enough to eat breakfast in the morning, let alone go to school. When he does

make it there, he's too busy containing his inner chaos to learn anything. (Unspoken truth: good-faith efforts are no substitute for a student-appropriate educational setting—but don't mess with The Budget, baby!)

If these things are happening to your family, like they have to mine, your child just might be "school-sick." If you've been reading around this book a bit you know by now there's a vast, virtual army of us. Incidents like the ones described above are ordinary events in the lives of mental health families, but their everydayness doesn't shield us from the pain and suffering they inflict. There are so many more (and more shocking) examples of the blows our kids and families absorb—striking painfully, every hour of every day of every school year.

Sometimes these injuries are cruelly intentional (more on that later). Sometimes, the intentions are pure. However, when your children are getting emotionally and/or physically hurt instead of legally, rightfully educated, you don't care much about good intentions. Or if you do, you need to get over that—*fast.*

Here's why: *you* can change your kid's life for the better, but only if you react bravely and firmly to the things happening, or not happening, at school. Only if you're willing to acknowledge good intentions when they exist—not to mention ill intent!—*but not settle for them.*

Knowledge + Skill = Power

Just because you've been dealt a few rotten hands in the Poker Game of Life doesn't mean game over. The lives we live—even when we've been socked with heartbreaking illnesses in our families—are at least partly under our own control. Winning or breaking even requires some combination of luck and skill. Not much you can do about luck, but skill? Sure you can! There may be a steep learning curve to this "education management" business—call it "school-healing" if you'd prefer—but you're a mental health parent. You're greater than any old learning curve.

Think of the school issue this way: your child languishing in an in-adequate school environment (or worse), on top of her disabling mental health conditions, is rotten luck. On the other hand, you know *a lot* about your kid's needs, probably more than you think you do. That's a net positive: you have knowledge, knowledge breeds skill, and knowledge + skill = power. You just need to figure out the variables that translate what you know and can do into real benefits for your child.

*Community + Curriculum + Teaching Modalities
+ Therapeutic Support = Healing*

One thing I've learned, living with, loving, and advocating for my own kids—and I believe this holds for all human beings, as well as many of our nonhuman friends and acquaintances—is that community is everything. If your child attends school in a social and learning environment that's inhospitable to *her*—forget how the other students are faring there—she will not "make it," by any honest measure. Just like us, our kids need to feel accepted and empowered if they are to succeed. Their ideal empowering environment should include the appropriate *people, curriculum, teaching modalities,* and *therapeutic framework* for a young person dealing with their specific challenges.

Of course, I can't tell each of you, readers, what *your* kid's ideal school environment, or therapeutic treatment, or medication regimen, or perfect nutritional intake would be—even though I can assure you these are all important factors and worth exploring. Like all human beings, our children are unique individuals, products of distinct environments and genetic combinations. Ultimately, while we can and should connect with each other via our parent networks to offer and receive mutual support, we will all have to do some personal heavy lifting on behalf of our own children.

I know my formulas work as a starting point. As I said, you're going to have to fill in the variables on your own, though. Help can come from friends and, crucially, professionals who know your child, the various educational options where you live, and any state or federal regulations that might affect your options.

THE NO-GUARANTEES GUARANTEE

There are no firm promises in life—especially in the lives of mental health families. Will finding the best school for your child make everything OK? I don't know, but there's a good chance it'll make things better than they were. Will healing his school-sickness cure your child's mental health disorder? No. At least, I've never heard of a genuine psychiatric illness that was cured simply by switching schools. There are so many moving parts here! If anything can solve all your problems, it's not solely this book and it's not one single school—even an awesome school. There are no guarantees, readers, except this: if you don't try—receiving and proffering assistance along the way—you can't make positive changes happen. It's in the trying that change starts and grows.

Stop! Before You Flunk Out Your Kid's School . . .

Try to divorce yourself from your emotional parts and look at the situation with clear eyes. As a parent, you've learned that a head cold is not bacterial meningitis is not cancer, and you respond to each illness accordingly—wait it out, call the pediatrician at midnight, race to the hospital in a panic, and so on. Well, "school-sickness" may be a tougher call. You'll probably face greater uncertainty and deeper confusion on all fronts (there's no blood test available—yet!). Still, just as you would with a medical illness, you'll need to make informed decisions about how you approach what's ailing your child.

This checklist should help you gain some perspective. Make sure you've mentally ticked off all the boxes below before concluding it's time to strap on your battle armor.

☐ *Be realistic.* Think of school the way a mature person thinks about a life partner: you're not getting it all, so sort out the must-haves and the can-do-withouts before you give up what you've got.

☐ *Be proactive.* If you sit around and wait for the school to do 100 percent right by your kid, you'll be sitting and waiting a long time—during which your child's needs will not be met. Even when it's all spelled out in writing and the folks involved are honorable and invested, some stuff you thought was agreed to simply won't get done unless you stay doggedly on top of things.

☐ *Be alert.* Lots of things happen (and don't happen) day to day at school that would hurt and surprise you. Don't count on your child, his teachers, or school administrators to fill you in. The school staff are busy. Some lack proper training and support. It can be easier (and far less costly, in the short term) to do the wrong thing—including withhold information. In plain English: education is about a lot of things besides a child's education and well-being. Budget, convenience, inflexible principles, stigma, ignorance, and, believe it or not, even retaliation against parents can all end up in that sausage. Make sure you remain in the loop. Take notes (or tape-record) all meetings and phone calls. Be sure you can prove you've tried (within reason) to work collaboratively with your school district to resolve any unacceptable issues.

☐ *Be adamant when you must.* There is *no legitimate reason* for a school district to delay honestly addressing a student's mental health or other serious challenges until that child has totally "crashed and burned" in some subpar school setting. Assume that there are unspoken "rules" governing how and when your district makes outside referrals, but not that these rules have legal standing—or that a school district's sluggish action on behalf of your child means a lack of appropriate alternatives. I will never totally forgive myself for standing by wringing my hands while one local school district slowly, agonizingly broke my beloved child, piece by piece—just because I didn't know we had options, and they made the less costly choice not to inform us.

☐ *If you're going to eat an elephant, do it one bite at a time.* I'm sorry, I had to add this. My dad says it to me when I'm feeling pulled in all directions at once and ready to flee. You know what, though? The mantra works. I even call Dad up sometimes and request he say it again. Hey, it quiets the chaos in my head—and it's free!

So. Have you tried being *realistic, proactive, alert, adamant,* and *eating your personal elephant one bite at a time,* but still believe your child is school-sick, or school is sick of your child? Have you tried in good faith to address the problems with your district? If so, then you need to start considering your other options.

Eight Questions to Get the Ball Rolling

1. Does your child get up most days willing and able to go to school?
2. Is he keeping up with homework and friendships?
3. Is she provided with necessary accommodations that address her mental health challenges, *and* making reasonable academic progress?
4. Do his teachers appreciate him—and *you*?
5. Does the school staff demonstrate understanding that no child exists in a vacuum and act accordingly—even when it's not their job to address the spread of school-related anguish throughout a student's family?
6. Are her teachers aware of her emotional disabilities and invested in helping her manage them?
7. Are the adults at school engaged and watchful?
8. Does he like and respect his classmates, and do they return the sentiments?

If the answer to all or most of these is yes, you've got something to celebrate! While your kid's school may not be perfect (what school is?) you can focus your energies, for now, on the nuts and bolts of learning and social stuff. Just don't let your guard down.

On the Other Hand . . .

1. Have behaviors at home changed markedly—for example, unusual aggression, fears, crying, anger, disrupted sleep patterns or appetite?
2. Has school-refusal intensified?
3. Do his stories about school seem weird or far fetched—or is he newly evasive when you ask questions?
4. Is there a perceptible drop in the quality and/or quantity of her schoolwork?

These emotional indicators, not to mention the most obvious physical red flags—unexplained bruises, swellings, contusions, and the like—can indicate things at school are gravely off kilter. Don't be afraid to demand information and accountability—especially if your child's communication skills prevent him from talking clearly about what's going on at school. And if you suspect your child is at risk, *don't* worry about false accusations or offended feelings! Too often we parents are the last to know what's really happening to our vulnerable kids. Our desire to please gets in the way of finding out.

Are you up to date on the state of corporal punishment in U.S. public schools? Check out what *Education Week* has to say on the subject:

"Twenty-nine states ban corporal punishment in public schools, but policies differ along geographic lines. Most of the 15 states in which laws explicitly permit this practice are located in the South and Southwest. In seven other states, laws do not refer to this form of discipline."[5]

When School Turns Perilous (Abuse Happens. What Then?)

For some parents, the problems laid out so far in this chapter will sound like much ado about nothing. That's because while many of us live in states where violent punishment by school staff is a crime, *some of us do not.*

In other words, *it might be legal, where you live, for teachers or school staff to beat and degrade your child at will.* This is neither a joke nor a bad dream. It's just the cruel reality in many of our fifty states. Students can be (and frequently are) paddled with a wooden instrument resembling a baseball bat, aggressively restrained, locked in closets for hours on end, publicly humiliated on the basis of their disabilities, and worse.

School abuse can and does happen anywhere, but in states where such things are "normal" and legally protected, it's that much harder for parents to keep their kids safe and protect the well-being of their families.

Here's the kicker: in states that legally endorse the use of corporal punishment, *physically and emotionally abusive measures are overwhelmingly used against students with disabilities.* Kids like yours and mine. According to the study, behaviors leading to these punishments are often disability related and beyond a student's control.

That is a desperate, scary situation for too many American kids and families—especially those without the time and mental focus to learn their legal rights, or the financial resources to hire an advocate or lawyer to help them fight the system. Still, there are actions parents can take, even in these extreme situations, to protect their kids from school-related trauma.

What Can You Do? Get Ready to Make a School Plan

School's not working out, but school in general is nonnegotiable. You can't pluck your child from the system at age fourteen and send him off to work (or up to his bedroom for the next four years), just because on days when Algebra 1 follows directly after PE he reliably has a full-blown panic attack. Or because it's only late November and he's already been hospitalized three times. You can't (it's illegal to withdraw from school at age fourteen), and you shouldn't, because the burger joint and/or his bedroom are not places where he's going to succeed without intervention, either. (If the situation is dangerous, though, act quickly to get him out of there, and plan your next steps afterward.)

On the off chance you're contemplating homeschooling—and who hasn't now and then—think carefully. Presumably, you're reading this book because you are deep in the trenches of mental health parenting. If the educators and clinicians who've given it a shot haven't been able to educate your child as she deserves, odds are you can't, either, unless you have 24/7 mental health counselors on staff—or you're willing to sacrifice the last vestiges of your own health and well-being in the process. I'm not saying the sacrifice wouldn't be worth it—I have no way to know. But I do know there would be sacrifice, and that sometimes the sacrifices we make on behalf of our children can impair our own health and well-being. If there's someone else who can take on the job and do it well, why not focus even just a bit on your body and psyche? You'll be a stronger and calmer parent if you take care of you.

As you take a hard look at your child's current education environment and explore alternative options, remind yourself that it's OK to reject a school that worsens your child's mental illness—especially after you've worked with the administration to try and make it better. In fact, it's essential. That goes even for the neighborhood school, the one your neighbors assured you is the Best. School. In. Town. Perhaps it is—for *their* kids. But that doesn't help yours.

If the thought of sniffing around classrooms, cafeterias, playgrounds, and athletic fields gets you nervous, and inquiring deeply into curricular issues, learning models, and social dynamics makes you queasy, you are not alone! But you can't fix what's broken if you don't take it apart and examine it, piece by piece. Lots of us have done it. Many will do it again and again. You can too!

Mental health parents aren't superheroes. We get it wrong more than we get it right. And we need help, the help of committed, compassionate adults, to raise kids with emotional disorders into flourishing grown-ups. Just remember this: effective mental health parenting requires the ultimate division of labor and knowledge. If I can assist with ideas for self-care, and strategies for getting through your day, it'll be another parent in your network who knows all the alternative school options for kids with certain disorders, or the name of a kick-ass, reasonably priced advocate who can help you. Others may be able to show you how to save money by prepping in advance for meetings with your advocate and school district. Still others will have the skinny on certain psych meds, or know something about your child's legal protections as a disabled minor (or young adult)—and so on. Not to mention the network of professionals you may have on your side.

It may take years of searching to find the right school for your child. Once you do, don't assume you're done! Your child's needs and the school's ability to address them can and will change—for better or for worse.

Making a School Plan

Remember your home plan from chapter 2, and your escape plan from chapter 3? A school plan can serve a similar purpose if you need to start "triage and treatment" of school-sickness. While my assumption here is that your child attends public school, your plan can certainly be modified to address a private school that's making your kid sick(er).

Please bear in mind that my advice regarding all things school should *only* be used alongside that of a trained professional who's familiar with special education law in your state, your school district, and the options available to a student with a profile like your child's. I can help you launch, but you need someone to keep you aloft.

1. REVIEW THE SITUATION

- Get involved with your public school district's Parent Advisory Council (PAC), sometimes called a Special Education Parent Advisory Council (SEPAC), if it has one. Learn about other people's experiences. Ask fellow special education parents for the lowdown on specific teachers and aides, specialized internal programs and curricula, and alternative (out-of-district) placements they may know about. Excellent connections can be made through the parents of your kid's schoolmates.
- Get your data ducks in a row. Request academic and psychological evaluations from the school if it's been a while since the last ones. Be sure to supplement those with outside evaluations by independent professionals (neuropsychological testing is a good place to start—the results of which may guide you toward other evals).
- Collect work samples from teachers. Don't let them off the hook: a sampling of your kid's schoolwork over time can tell all kinds of stories.
- Request diagnostic letters from your kid's mental health clinician(s), as well as notes and discharge summaries from psychiatric hospitalizations. But do make sure clinicians are clearly informed about everything going on in school as well as at home, so they can effectively help advocate for a better educational placement for your child.
- Be *that parent*. Show the special education director and other school staff you're no doormat, and that you understand your child and her educational rights under federal and state law. (Just make sure you've done your research beforehand—or even better, consulted with a good advocate.) You may end up with a reputation as one of *those impossible parents*, but you're here to help your kid, not earn "favorite family" status among the administration; play it too nice and they may walk all over you.

- Zero in on your kid's most urgent needs. Emotional healing with on-demand therapy and medication management? Academic focus with appropriate supports? A more hospitable general environment? How about 24/7 programming? You probably won't find them all rolled up in one package—and your child's first move into an alternative placement will likely not be the last. When Ben left public school in fifth grade, it was primarily for the purpose of healing. We didn't care much about academics at that time; we just wanted to keep him alive through his adolescent years. Later, while enrolled at his third out-of-district school (which would be next to last), he let us know us he'd healed enough to learn. Once again we got to searching for a new and better placement. Luckily, we found it!

2. TAKE A NEXT STEP—RESOURCES TO MOVE YOU FORWARD

- Take a look at the U.S. Department of Education (www.ed.gov) website for information on current special education law and other important issues. If you can, bookmark this page and keep an eye on it. Depending on factors such as who sits in the secretary of education's chair, things change. Also, keep tabs on your state's DOE website. These sites should be among your go-to resources. Other excellent websites include:
  - Wrightslaw (www.wrightslaw.com), a one-stop shop for all things special education (SPED) law
  - the Federation for Children with Special Needs (https://fcsn.org/), which offers broad-based information and resources for parents of kids with all kinds of disabilities
  - the National Association for Parents with Children in Special Education (http://www.napcse.org/)
  - National Council on Independent Living (https://www.ncil.org/)

These are just a few of the resources available. Fire up Dr. Google when you're ready to look for more.

- Research therapeutic, special needs schools in your local or regional area. Ask your SEPAC community, Facebook groups, and other networks for suggestions. Read online reviews (with a grain of salt). Do a Google search for lawsuits and citations against the schools on your list—as well any other information that will offer a view into their inner workings. And don't forget: an advocate or educational consultant can be an invaluable resource.

- Make a short list of potential candidates.
- Call them up and ask to speak to an administrator about their academic and therapeutic programming, student body profile, enrichments, and so on.
- Request a list of parent references. When you contact parents, ask for brutal honesty and lob some hard questions at them—especially given what you know about the potential for abuse in schools. If a school tells you they "never connect prospective parents with current parents," take it as a red flag. (Don't ever assume that just because a school has dedicated itself to educating children with severe emotional disabilities there's no abuse or incompetence on its grounds.)
- For each prospect, write up a list of pros and cons. So hokey, right? But the pros-and-cons list is a classic, proven life tool—there's a reason your mom and dad used to make you use it. (The model below is meant for illustration only; as with my formulas a few pages back, your variables will depend on your child, your family circumstances, and what's available to you.)

Pros:
- ○ Low student-to-teacher ratio
- ○ Small class size
- ○ Appropriate peers (seemingly)
- ○ Specialized staff training
- ○ On-site therapy/med management
- ○ Animal therapy
- ○ College and/or vocational prep
- ○ Day (or residential) option

Cons:
- ○ Loss of connection to the local community
- ○ Long commute
- ○ Extra costs (possibly including tuition and fees)
- ○ Transportation logistics and expense
- ○ Loss of certain electives—art, music, sports
- ○ Boarding away from home (could also be placed in the "Pro" column)

Pros-and-cons lists like this can help you wrangle with tough life decisions. Still, don't be surprised when you find yourself evaluating the merits/demerits of small class size versus long commute versus animal therapy. They may appear (maddeningly) to cancel each other out, but at some point, the scales will tip in one direction or another. Make ample use of your parent networks and professional/clinical supports as you work through your list.

3. TAKE ANOTHER COUPLE OF STEPS

You've gathered your data (evaluations, work samples, clinician letters, etc.); consulted your networks and, ideally, a good advocate; ushered in Dr. Google for research assistance; made a short list and a pros-and-cons table; and contacted prospective schools for information. You're certain things at the current school aren't going to get better and could hardly be worse. It's time to do the following:

- Prepare to make a compelling case for a placement change to your child's special education team. (I'm assuming your child has an Individualized Education Plan [IEP] in her public school . . . if not, or if your child is already in a private school, you'll probably be doing this on your own—and financing it too. Just skip this part, apply directly to schools, and figure out your own method of financing.)
- Bring in a special education advocate if you've managed to hire one.
- Request a team meeting to discuss changing your child's placement.

4. ALLOW YOURSELF SOME SELF-DOUBT

You will doubt everything. You will feel overwhelming relief. You will blame yourself for ruining your kid's life. You will be tempted to phone the special education director and call it off. Just sit with those feelings—they're normal. Acknowledge the hard work you've done to this point and try to relax. If you believe in your child, let him know you've got his back, and stay involved; odds are, it'll work out. You might have to adjust your perspective a bit to accommodate different visions of success, but in my opinion, the whole world would benefit from that exercise. Don't think of redefining success to match the person your child actually *is* as a letdown or a loss—differences of every kind are what makes life beautiful and exciting.

It would be irresponsible of me not to acknowledge those tragic cases where things go very wrong. In a minority of cases, our kids don't make it. Our families are irreparably broken. The families of others may be trapped with us in that terrible storm of pain. Children pass in and out of our domestic circles—emotionally and geographically. Lives end, sometimes as anticipated, sometimes with a great shock of surprise. Always with wrenching anguish.

In some cases, we simply can't subdue these troubled psyches over the long term. But much more often, we manage them well enough to keep our families intact and sustain some forward motion.

No one can guarantee things will work out the way you hope and dream; that goes for every human being, with or without mental illness, who dwells on this earth. But there's no reason to assume that your love and fierce advocacy won't make a big difference in your child's life. In fact, the odds are on your side. Just keep fighting, readers!

PROFESSIONAL FYI: LET'S TALK ADVOCATES!

Cynthia Moore, a Massachusetts-based special needs advocate with her own family history of mental health disorders, offers five reasons why you should hire a professional special education advocate:

1. *Advocates* bring advocates to their kids' IEP meetings. Why? Same reason surgeons don't operate on their own kids: the stakes are too high. Every oppositional or derogatory comment from your school district can feel like a personal insult. While you're dealing with blow after blow, you're not thinking critically about the situation. You're forgetting what you know about your child's rights, neglecting to look at your notes, or failing to recall that crucial point the school counselor recently made about your child's emotional impairment. Your own emotions literally impair your ability to listen, organize your thoughts, and effectively advocate for your child. You're in "fight or flight" mode. That adrenaline might help when you're about to be mauled by a bear, but not so much when you're negotiating with your school district.

2. You'll want a witness to what transpired. If you're left with no choice but to take legal measures to ensure your child's

needs are met, you can't very credibly serve as your own witness—even if you've recorded all of your meetings (don't skip the recording, though, even with an advocate on hand).

3. Advocates know the process, and ideally, the internal culture within school districts. Are the administrators easygoing, lawsuit minded, vengeful? Does the district have a reputation for serial violations of special education laws? They also speak the language of special education. Yes, it matters *how* you inform your district that you're removing your kid from public school. You might believe you can unenroll your child, pay out of pocket for a more suitable, private placement, and go back to sue the district four years later to recoup your expenses. A good advocate can tell you why that won't work—and help you handle things the right way, so your child's interests are served, and you don't lose your shirt in the process.

4. An ethical advocate will know when you need the services of a lawyer, and refer you to some she's worked with in the past. If you're worried about the cost of a legal battle over your child's education, ask her advice on how to save money. There's a lot of preparation work you can do on your own, no law degree required—and the more you do, the less you'll be paying a professional to do for you. Just don't forget: advocates, in general, are not lawyers, do not practice law, and do not offer legal advice.

5. Special education advocacy is an unregulated profession, so buyer, beware! What you need is an *experienced, qualified advocate*. A bad one can do you more harm than good. Make sure you do your homework before putting any deposit on the table. Ask, before you hire:

   - For details on their training and *ongoing* continuing education
   - About active engagements with national, state, and/or local advocacy groups and committees
   - What they consider their strengths (e.g., written and verbal communication, translation of tricky or specialized concepts to laypeople, strong emotional intelligence, special education [SPED] policy expertise, etc.). Look for an advocate

whose strengths will complement yours, and compensate for your weaknesses.

- How they deal with the emotional hurt experienced by parents in negotiations with their school district, while maintaining a rational, fact-based approach to the situation before them
- About their fluency in state *and* federal law. Choose a specialist (practices in your state only) over a generalist (practices in multiple states)—deep knowledge is more beneficial to *your* case than broad.
- Finally, be aware that most states do *not* consider communication between advocate and client to be privileged. Make sure you ask your potential advocate about the situation where you live, and how he or she deals with supporting and protecting clients accordingly.[6]

OUR STORY: SNAPSHOTS #9–#12

School has been an eternal challenge for our family. Ben went from disaster to disaster—public elementary school, to a public special needs middle school, to a hopeful but problematic private day school, to a first-good-then-awful residential school in a neighboring state, and finally to his current (excellent) placement: a private boarding school for bright kids with emotional impairments. The day-to-day misery of feeling educationally homeless and helpless, a stranger in his neighborhood schools, almost killed him—and me.

Snapshot #9. October 25, 2011

Sixth grade, and Benjy is currently without a placement. Public school made him want to end his life. He'd leave the house marginally whole, and return home broken. Although he is super bright, he has mostly learned on his own. Classrooms are too stressful for learning, full of noise and unexpected demands and social unreliability.

What did public school ever do for him, except teach him the practices of self-loathing and self-harm? Oh, right. It gave him a chance to learn the inner geographies and systems of some locked psychiatric units, by launching him directly into them.

Now, we are caught in the sorry space between the toxic school and a hopeful one. The hopeful school, which is on the campus of an important psychiatric hospital, seemed perfect to Ben on his daylong visit today—a locked-down, stimulus-free paradise.

Lars and I have been fighting to send our small boy, not quite twelve years old, to school at a *mental hospital*. We've been praying they'll accept him, and our school district will honor its legal obligation and send him there, because he must go to school, and he must live. We need those two things, not necessarily in that order, from the universe.

When Ben emerged from his trial classes today, we heard his chatty voice before we even saw him. When he came into view, his body seemed relaxed, his face bright. It's possible he heard and retained some interesting bit of knowledge in there. Something more lively than a new vocabulary word, or a math fact. He might even have felt a little happiness.

Once not long ago, just for kicks, I tried to pinpoint the last time Ben had experienced pleasure, or something like it, in school, and what I came up with was: never. Not once. Not even an hour of it. There might have been minutes or even hours of *not traumatized*, but as far as I can tell, no *happy*.

Today he may have felt it. He's begging to start tomorrow. (*What??*) I'm just sitting around biting my nails, picking my cuticles, and waiting for an email saying, *Benjamin! Welcome to Our Little School*! I expect it may come tomorrow. Also, I definitely expect to be disappointed.

Snapshot #10. October 27, 2011

Benjy is a person of leisure and not a schoolchild at present—still waiting for the mental hospital school to decide if he's . . . what, good enough? bad enough? to let in. It's insane how often this happens to kids like Ben: they must leave one school before another, safer or better one, can be secured. I pray there's no chain of rejections ahead.

He is bored out of his mind and anxious because he knows he's in limbo. He started his day with *Prehistoric Park* on Netflix. Then he got restless, and restless was soon followed by agitated.

Then we descended into the cranky, desperate consumerism that is what a mixed manic episode looks like in my child.

"I really need an Xbox. Everyone has at least one. I know if you got me just that one thing I'd be happy, it's not all that much, and anyway I have no school!" I knew what was coming next. Escalate, escalate, pace, pace, pace, cry, get some rage on, collapse in despair, go buy the Xbox. What else could we do? Anything to avert a full-blown crisis.

On our drive to the big-box store, Benjy asked me about the Occupy Wall Street movement, which has been all over the news.

"What exactly *is* Wall Street, and why does it have to be occupied?"

"Oh, I can tell you *all* about that!" I said, perking up. Oh, boy. I never, ever learn from previous stupid mistakes. My War-on-Wall-Street threw Ben into despair. He draped my jacket over his head and curled into a fetal position. He told me through my jacket that life is not worthwhile, that it holds no treasures for him. Little I could do to lure him back from the deep of his own misery.

We braved the icy rain that had begun pelting the car. We picked up an Xbox, and then Saskia from school.

Things flip around here. Moods, coins, kids on trampolines, pancakes on Lars's spatula. My kids are in the basement, racing cars or flying planes or walking on the moon, for all I know. I hear laughter from where I'm sitting.

Snapshot #11. December 20, 2011

The Hopeful School, two months in and a decent start. But Ben's not at school today. When I woke him at seven he complained of a severe cough. And he *is* coughing quite a bit. But with Ben you never know whether a somatic complaint is actually a psychiatric one. So here I am, analyzing my boy, searching for clues. Is he hot? His forehead feels cool. Is he listless? A little, especially when I ask him to try to rouse himself and go to school.

No illness flares without suspicion in homes like mine. A headache is a headache is creeping depression. Stomach pains are too many french toast sticks. Or else, a panic attack.

We've had a few setbacks of late. Nothing extreme. No shredded fingertips or bloodstained clothes. His lower lip is scabby and swollen, but that's baseline now. Still. There've been a few nights before, and mornings of, when he's pleaded with me to let him stay home from school. And recently, a full sleepless night, complete with a "relax bath" in the wee hours, that brought back some heavy memories.

So, I wonder what's going on. Ben tells me he's opted out of two field trips recently, one to a bank and the other to a library. I have a theory about these opt-outs. I think he's anxious about the unpredictable behaviors of his classmates, and how those might play out in public. He has never dealt well with unpredictability or disruptiveness in other kids. And right now there's a boy in his class who struggles with containing his emotions, is aggressive and volatile—sometimes toward Ben. Maybe today's bodily complaint is a protest against the unpredictable and the disruptive at school. I just can't know for sure because that is not something Benjy would fess up to.

So here we are at home, and all I can do is keep him off the computer for as long as possible and tell him if he's too sick for school he's too sick for screen time. And keep my fingers crossed we're not in for another storm.

Snapshot #12. January 23, 2012

Less than four months at school and the old mental illnesses are back with a vengeance. With the short, dark days, depression and anxiety always return. We had hoped, and even believed those days were over. Fool us once, fool us twice. Fool us a few score times more.

These days, Ben can't leave his bed and face the world without promises of junk food and computer games. Even the Hopeful School is a scary place, now, although he still claims he loves it.

Benjy is a mass of contradictions. A boy who's one way on Wednesday morning and a completely different person by Wednesday afternoon. He *loves* chicken noodle soup—he gobbled some up just last night—but as of now he *hates* that stuff and can't get it down without gagging. He loves school hates school loves school. He has a friend, yet he is friendless.

It's dizzying, keeping it all straight. I'm parenting a child who's a moving target. Sure, all kids are variable; all of them grow and change. But kids like Benjy can't settle into themselves; they can't rest. They are always roiling, always in flux. It must be *hard* being Benjy. And in some ways, although he is my perfect treasure, it's hard to be his mother. I'm desperate to help him. To cure his pain. Make life easier for him. And those are things I simply can't do. Not yet. Maybe not ever.

I can love him and be there for him. Make sure his school is working for him, get him his meds, and confirm they are the right ones. I can take him to therapy and his psychiatrist, try to help him maintain his few friendships. Look ceaselessly for opportunities for him. Things he can do and be successful at. Things he can do and enjoy. There are not a whole lot of those yet, but I keep trying.

We got Ben out the door today. Lars drove him to the Hopeful School. Late, because he was struggling this morning, and needed to sit under his seasonal affective disorder light for a while.

I'm just waiting for the call I know is coming. I have papers to grade and teaching notes to write, but I've got to hold off because I know the call is coming, and once my concentration's broken it's gone for the day. They won't make me drive there and pick him up unless he is wrecked and *has* to go, but they'll call me to let me know he's fragile and falling apart. And then my day will be about him. Worrying and thinking desperately about how I can make things change, and what change starts with—school, meds, or something we've never yet thought of.

Sometimes I think true maturity is accepting that there are things you won't ever be able change and maintaining your equanimity in the face of that. I hope I live to know that kind of peace.

HER THERAPEUTIC SCHOOL GOT IT SO WRONG: ANNABELLA AND MAGGIE'S STORY

In chapter 2, Annabella described the challenges of keeping teenage daughter Maggie safe at home. Here she tells me about the "therapeutic" program that only made things much worse.

Annabella: After Maggie was discharged from her first hospitalization she was placed in a new program at her high school, a so-called therapeutic classroom with built-in therapy and emotional supports. We were happy, at least, that our district made an effort to address her issues and help her regain her footing at school.

But . . . these people really did not seem to know what they were doing. Every fifteen minutes they would interrupt whatever she was doing and make her rate her suicidal feelings on a scale of one to ten. Can you imagine? Nothing like constant reminders, in case you forgot you wanted to kill yourself. They said it was because they didn't know her yet. You think they might find a better way to get inside her head than bombarding her with, "Are you feeling suicidal? How would you rate your sadness, on a scale of one to ten?"

So, no great surprise, she starts escalating. They call me up and tell me to come to school right away. When I get there, they've got her in a room with a teacher and the school counselor, and she's pacing. Just pacing, and I can see the agitation. The counselor tells me he thinks I should call mobile crisis, which basically sends a team of mental health clinicians to assess a kid's condition and initiate the hospitalization process if needed.

Well, forty-five minutes go by as we wait for mobile crisis, and that whole time this guy keeps asking her, "Do you think you're safe? Are you at risk of self-injury or suicide right now?" and everything amps up. I feel in my bones he's not doing this right—that this forty-five-minute delay would be better used for distraction. Breathing exercises, whatever. Because sometimes they come back down if you give them the mental space to do it.

Anyway, finally she's had enough and she gets up and walks out the door of this room they've got us in. She doesn't say anything, just walks out quietly and goes about twenty feet to the end of the hall where there's an exit door. And she just stands there looking out.

The counselor thought this was an emergency, and I thought, *You know, I don't blame her for wanting to get out of there. I get it.* But he told me he was calling an ambulance, better not wait for mobile crisis anymore. He said she looked like she wanted to run out into traffic.

Now mind you, these doors looked out onto a parking lot. All parked cars, no traffic. And also, I may be new to parenting a teen with mental illness—because these issues all came on so suddenly, out of nowhere—but I think I know my child. And I pushed back on the ambulance. It was hard, but I said, "I don't actually think this is an emergency. Please don't call."

Long story short, we went back to that room, and while we continued waiting, they gave her some playdough and she kneaded and massaged it. I could literally watch her decompressing. When mobile crisis finally arrived, they interviewed each of us privately—Maggie, me, the school counselor—and their opinion was, this does not rise to the level where we'd admit her. She'd just been inpatient for seven weeks, and they felt it would be better for her to receive intensive outpatient and home-based services, which they could help arrange.

I wish I had just taken her home with me right then, just walked out behind the crisis team. But you know how it is, it's hard to think straight, and you want to defer to people you think have more experience than you. . . . I mean, you're *desperate* for someone to know more about this crap than you, so you take their word as the last truth. So, we waited on the school to see what they said. That counselor was so freaked out by her—he obviously had no effing clue—that he called an ambulance against my wishes. All the while Mags is escalating again. Every time he asks her if she feels safe, what do you think she says? *No.* What kid *would* feel safe there?

This was a nightmare. I felt we had to get on the ambulance because the ball was rolling now. We spent eight hours in the ER, and Maggie had to go through those usual indignities . . . pee in a cup, blood test, no privacy, invasive questions. The worst part of the whole experience, though, was when these two mean ladies came in; they were social workers from the Department of Children, Youth, and Families (the agency that investigates neglect and abuse cases), and they accused her of manipulating the system. They said she had a boyfriend in the hospital and she wanted to get back in to see him. They left us alone, and she tried to sleep. But later they came barging into the room, banged on the wall, flipped the light on, and said, "Get up! You're not here to sleep. We're gonna talk."

They fired a bunch of questions at her. "Are you bullied?" "Are you using drugs?" "Do you have a boyfriend?" "Is there violence in your home?" "Does your father live in the home with you? Do you get along with him?" After they'd finished with all these aggressive questions, they said again that she was being manipulative to get into the hospital. Not only that, but they kind of accused *me* of having the wool pulled over my eyes. I told them we were only there because the school made us go!

And then they tried to scare us. "Look," they said, "we don't think she needs to be in the hospital, but if we fill out this form and say she needs hospitalization we're going to send her to"—these were their exact words—"a dirty CBAT [community-based acute treatment facility] in the city. So bad you will sleep in your car in the parking lot because you won't want to leave her there."

Can you even imagine someone would say something like that?

Last thing they said was, "So, Maggie, do you feel safe enough to go home, or we going to hospitalize you?" Obviously, she chose home. Took off that stupid johnny and put on her jeans and her UGG boots, and we got out of there. We were so exhausted and shaken, we cried together all the way home. People think they're being helpful, you know? And sometimes they just make things so much worse.

OPEN MIC: KIDS SPEAK OUT

Webster, Age Twenty, New York

I had a lot of issues in school. I was in public school through tenth grade. There was way too much homework, in my opinion, and it started back in elementary school. Too much stress. It all ramped up my anxiety. I kind of felt like, honestly? the school couldn't care less about me—about who I was as a person. They cared about the output. Like, I amounted to how many pages I read and math problems I did the night before, and how many mistakes I made or didn't make on my tests. No one noticed I was losing it, and nobody bothered to ask about anything but my output.

My last day in public school was the day I started throwing chairs. Man, I still can't believe I did that. Well, they noticed me! All those years of no support, no "How are you doing today, Webster, do you need anything from us? Do you want to talk?" And there wasn't any of it after the chairs, either, 'cause they were scared of me. Which I don't really blame them. So, yeah, they banned me from that school, I went to the hospital, and when I came out, my mom and dad had arranged for a new school, a private school for kids of my "type"—I have Asperger's and depression.

The new school was better in a lot of ways. They did offer emotional support, but it was the opposite of public school . . . so much "emotional support" it felt intrusive. Looking back, I wish I could have found a happy medium. Either way, you feel misunderstood, like they've mistaken you for some other kid. A needier kid or a less needy one. I think school would have been a better experience for me if my teachers had just tried harder to know me. I probably could have self-advocated better, and that's something I've been working on. I'm in college now, and it's been up and down. It's obviously not a therapeutic environment, but at least I've found other students who are on my wavelength. That helps. I don't know what happens after I graduate, though. I'm trying to take it one day at a time.

THE TAKEAWAY

- If your child is "school-sick," it may be time for a change in placement.
- Don't ever view ditching public school—or any school that isn't working for your kid—as a failure on his part or yours. The *system* is failing *him*. You're simply doing what needs to be done to make things right. With diligence, watchfulness, and determined advocacy for your child, there's a good chance you'll succeed—even if it takes a few more school changes to find the program that meets his needs.
- For your school district's administrators, all roads lead to The Budget. Don't automatically assume decisions made on your child's behalf are in your child's best interest. They might be, but stay closely involved.
- Corporal punishment is alive and well in certain (mostly southern) states. Students with disabilities suffer disproportionately from it.
- A *school plan* can help you figure out whether your kid's school is a keeper—and if not, how to move forward with your plan B.
- Because a change of educational placement can have complications (and be financially ruinous if you're on the hook for private tuition), *hire a good special education advocate, if you can.*

- Make your best case for a school change, if you expect your school district's support. You'll need a battery of recent independent evaluations, including (but not limited to) neuropsychological, psychological, and academic testing.
- On top of whatever federal law pertains to special education (SPED) at any given moment, each state also has its own regulations and protocols. Make sure you—or your advocate, at least—know about federal and state laws and regulations.
- Negotiating with your school district without professional support would be like a weekend checkers player (you) challenging Garry Kasparov to a game of chess. Don't.

5

MAINTAINING YOUR HEALTHY RELATIONSHIPS, DITCHING THE TOXIC ONES

Ever felt like you're alone on an ice floe at the world's end, with nothing but a great chilly void between you and the horizon? I have. I'm quite accomplished in the art of feeling lonely in a crowd. I could be with husband, friends, family, strangers—no matter. When my inner life is awash with anxiety and grief and I'm so overwhelmed I can't see or hear anything outside my own thumping fear, my tendency is to shut down.

Unfortunately, that's not a winning strategy unless you're a tortoise, or maybe a hedgehog. Tuning out those around you and pretending "there's nothing to see here" doesn't change your reality, it simply blocks off natural pathways to community and support.

The only thing harder than caring for a self-harming, seriously dysregulated kid is trying to do it alone: friendless, bereft of partnership and moral support. Plenty of single parents raise kids with psychiatric illnesses, and do so with great courage and success. But the ones who do best have found support in friends, family, and their parent networks. They clearly understand the power of human connection, and work at sustaining their mutually satisfying relationships.

I believe in the life-enhancing power of human relationships too. It took some doing, but I've mostly conquered that impulse to withdraw from the world when *my* world starts imploding. I'm grateful I did! If you haven't yet learned to do the same, get going; it's never too late to start.

FIVE THINGS I WISH I KNEW FROM THE BEGINNING

1. It's hard to open up about mental illness—the stigma is real. But so is the capacity, in good people, to sympathize with your challenges

105

and respond with compassion. The pros of disclosure to people you care about usually outweigh the cons, hands down.

2. Just because statistics show that more marriages than not implode under the weight of disability parenting, *doesn't mean yours will.* It's possible to emerge from the cruelest of circumstances still joined at the hip, even if a bit bruised.

3. Occasionally, you'll choose to suck it up when family and close friends behave insensitively around you and/or your kid, and that is OK. Accepting the challenge of educating them about childhood mental illness is a noble, worthwhile effort, but it's *not* an obligation.

4. Sometimes your effort to educate the ignorant is not worthwhile. Figure out the difference and be prepared to cut those people loose.

5. If anything can save your marriage, friendships, and other relationships, it's good, honest communication. Tell the people who matter what you need from them, and ask them what they need from you. Work at it. And remember: relationships are a two-way street.

YOU'RE TIRED. DO YOU HAVE TO?

I'm tired too. I feel your killer fatigue. And maintaining a circle of loved ones and friends takes energy, which is always in short supply. Still, I think you ought to grit your teeth and do it. Read on and I'll tell you why.

Not only does it take physical energy to manage your relationships, but you've also got to exercise your emotional intelligence (EI) muscles. *Quality* human interactions require the ability to step outside oneself and enter some other person's experience—even if only by absorbing their words and responding accordingly with words of one's own.

It's a lot of work, but it's worth the effort.

Life for mental health families is hard enough without tossing a heaping cup of loneliness into the mix. Cultivating and tending relationships requires the same kind of care you'd take with a garden, if only you had time for gardening. Plants grow and blossom if you water them the proper amount, notice which species thirst after sunshine and which prefer shade, apply the right type of fertilizer, and pluck out invasive weeds. You can manage this: it's not brain surgery.

Think of your human relationships as a mixed garden of hardy, sun-loving blooms and shy shade-seekers. Pithy grasses, delicate ornamentals, and tenacious vines and creepers. Or, if you're not up for dealing in metaphor today (and honestly, who could blame you?), just think of it like this: You've got people in your life who will be there for you and lend support no matter what. You've got others who, though perfectly pleasant folks, *don't actually want to hear how it's goin'* when they say, "Hey, how's it goin'?" And I'll bet anything you've got some of those vines and creepers among your friends, whose sole purpose seems to be to choke you and take you down.

You've got to learn how to tell these species apart, assess how important they are in your life, and act accordingly. To whom can you confide your most personal, sometimes dark, secrets and sorrows, without compromising your relationship? Which relatives and friends get to see the real you (greasy hair, chewed nails, eye bags, black humor, and all) and which ones get the G-rated version of you—the abridged (OK, fake) "Everything's fine, we're doing great, school's a bit more challenging this year but on the bright side I'm seeing a *lot* more of Brianna these days!" edition. And who, among the folks in your orbit, are the toxic ones—the relationships you really ought to weed out?

You may feel resistant to these suggestions. I don't blame you if you do. It's damned *hard* to be social when your life is exhausting, depressing, impossible to explain. When it's so far from "typical" human experience, you might as well not bother trying.

Unlike most others in your family or circle of friends, *your* child may or may not survive to adolescence, may or may not wake tomorrow to a paranoid, parallel reality. So, how on earth are you supposed to listen to Aunt Millie go on about her crappy veins, or endure your cousin Frank's obsessing over his daughter's chance for a full athletic scholarship to FML University?

But forget about Aunt Millie and Cousin Frank! How can you possibly do all those things "normal" wives and husbands and life partners do? Can you really abandon yourself to the joys of intimacy with your partner—physical, conversational, emotional fun—without feeling you're betraying your suffering kid, mentally checking in on where he is now, how he was doing last time you saw him, and which shoe will be the next to drop? Is discussing finances and divvying up household tasks without panic rising and anger flaring even a *thing*? Those simple acts (the intimacy, the fun, the budgeting, the cleaning of the marital bathroom) were the sort of things you signed up for when you got married, unless you signed up for some alternative plan. But they may seem beyond reach now that your job includes protecting a child you love from the dangers of her own psyche. Sometimes there is just no clear space in your *own* psyche to focus on anyone or anything else except that young life in need of protection.

Same goes for your most treasured friendships. When nine-tenths of your waking life is spent anguishing over the illness that's taken root in your family, and nine-tenths of theirs is not, why even go through the motions of connecting with those friends who knew you before you were living this way?

I don't pretend to have any definitive solutions to these problems. I know of no foolproof plan for saving those relationships worth saving. But my own life experience, therapy work, and emotional intelligence tells me this: as hard as it is to enjoy a lighthearted night out with your friends, surrender yourself to good sex, or take care of your needs in any enthusiastic way while your child is ill and vulnerable to self-harm, practicing these actions can be like exercising a wasted muscle. It can make you stronger and healthier. Positive relationships are crucial to our well-being. Why? Because humans are not built for solitude, or for bearing our internal burdens without emotional assistance. We need that shoulder to cry on, the listening ear, the friendly, open heart. Chances are, we already had some of those in our lives as we began our transition to parenthood. Why let them fizzle out when we need them more than ever?

You can bolster and reclaim those fizzled relationships—marital, platonic, extended family—by paying attention to your own needs *and* the inner lives of others.

Not all of them, of course. But the ones you want and need in your life. Here's what that can look like in practice: say I know my son Ben is safe at school, doing well lately, and in no imminent danger of crisis—even though he's been talking about going off his meds and joining the Marines when he turns eighteen. I'm sitting with my hypothetical great-aunt Millie, and she's feeling sorry for herself. Her legs hurt. I make myself listen to her describe her pain, with an open mind and no judgment—exactly the way I wish to be heard when I choose to speak about my anguish. Of a sudden, I recognize our kinship: I don't have problem veins, but boy, do I have pain in my legs—almost all the time. If I listen to her words, watch her gestures (Is she rubbing them while she speaks? Does she seem to be wearing support hose?), I can chime in with sympathy, and even tell her about my own hurt. Do her legs ache in bed, like mine do? Does she elevate them during the day? Is walking worse than rest?

The payoff for me is, I'm given the gift (yes, gift!) of focusing on someone and something else, rather than my usual themes of bipolar disorder, suicidality, financial stress, and my own waning health. I get dragged out of my self-absorption and placed into an active posture of helping someone I care about. The payoff for Aunt Millie is she's relieved for an hour or two of her pain because she has someone to sympathize and make her feel heard.

Between us, we have the power to turn monologue into dialogue, and pointless pain into productive interaction.

Maybe there's a backstory here. Maybe when I was a little girl she always had a Hershey bar or two somewhere, and they somehow found their way into my hands when I wasn't watching. Perhaps she liked to stroke my hair, and when I told her it felt good, she kept at it as long as I needed her touch.

Why wouldn't I make the effort to keep Aunt Millie a sympathetic figure in my life, rather than allowing her quirks to irritate me and close me off to her? Now, if my kid was suicidal that day and Pretend Aunt Millie called to complain about her veins, I'd have to rebuff her. Likely, she would know the context, hear the panic in my voice, and say, *Go!* If she just started talking and I hung up on her, she'd most likely accept my explanation later (and maybe pop a chocolate bar in the mail to make amends).

What I've just described is fairly simple. With a person you want to keep in your life:

- Tune in.
- Find your point of contact (if one exists).
- Engage, which can transform a *"talking at"* situation to a *"talking with"* one.

These are tacks you can take in person, on the phone, via email, and even via text (unless you have fuzzy eyesight and klutzy fingers, like me, in which case you'll want to avoid using texts for important emotional work).

Here's how I might approach the situation with my hypothetical cousin Frank and his star athlete daughter:

- Try hard to suppress my irritation at his "privileged problems"—and remember, he's family
- Tune in to the spoken and the unspoken: higher education is insanely expensive. His much-loved daughter has a shot at a scholarship at her "perfect" college. If she doesn't get one, Frank will have to choose between breaking her heart and cracking into his hard-earned but insufficient retirement savings—a real chance of serious pain and sacrifice.
- Realize that *I know those feelings*, albeit in different contexts
- Instead of thinking, *Yeah, boo-hoo*, tell him I feel his pain, and show him how our situations are not all that different

I tend my relationship with Frank by listening openly and expressing my sense of shared experience (even if I secretly still think *I* was dealt the harder hand). I draw him into my own internal life while accepting the authenticity of his, and we both gain from it. Next time he calls, maybe he'll ask about *my* struggles first. At the very least, he'll anticipate a reciprocal connection over the pain and heartbreak that can accompany parenting.

The bottom line: for most people, life is better when shared. We're social beings by nature, and with some exceptions—every rule has exceptions—we dread isolation. Sure, parenting a child with significantly disordered health or development can make social connectedness harder. It can break friendships and loveships. It can fracture families and destroy professional relationships. But no one said you can't buck the trend and maintain successful connections with the people you depend on.

Relationship Breakdown 101: Common Symptoms and Sensible Solutions

Think things are "normal" with partner, friends, family? They may be. But what if your status quo is dysfunctional? Here are some signs that mental health parenting is negatively impacting your relationships:

1. *Symptom:* Verbal and physical intimacy with your partner has dried up. The thought of intimacy makes you anxious or aggravated. Good conversation? Good sex? What are those?

   Solutions:
   - Talk about it. Stuff like that festers when it's not addressed, and festering ills can poison a marriage or life-partnership. Explain why all you want to do in bed is sleep, untouched. (If it helps, chronically deficient sleep, a junky diet, and those daily cortisol cocktails you drink would make even Gisele Bundchen feel unsexy. You may quote me on that.)
   - Invite your partner to tell his or her side of the story. Ask for help in brainstorming solutions to the problem.
   - Commit to showing interest in your partner, no matter how frazzled you feel. Ask about his or her day, and if the interest isn't reciprocal, volunteer something positive about yours. I know it's hard to look up from your Facebook groups—those sanity-preserving networks of sisters and brothers in adversity—but your partner can play the role of sanity saver too, if you show

him or her how. First, though, you have to make some serious emotional contact.

- Don't forget to tend to your own need to be recognized and cared for. If your partner doesn't return your gestures of connection, tell him or her your feelings are important too—and suggest ways to satisfy them. My repertoire of nudges includes, "Would you like to hear about my day too? I'd love to share it with you!" And, "It would feel so good if you'd offer to make me a cup of tea right now! I could really use some TLC."
- Reintroduce touch: gently squeeze his elbow; brush the hair off her brow. Place a hand on his knee; kiss her ear. The tiniest physical gestures can make you feel like partners again—and baby steps have a way of extending into long strides.
- A well-timed smile, or a hug, will go a long way toward taking down defenses—yours and theirs.
- Invest in couple's therapy. This *could* be the best thing you do for yourselves—if it's done right. (Make sure the focus is on listening, sharing, empathizing, and allowing yourselves to be vulnerable. If all you do is criticize each other, you will end up with both your noses out of joint.) Therapy doesn't have to be a long-term commitment . . . you can learn the skills you need to keep your marriage afloat in a handful of sessions, and incorporate them into your lives.

2. *Symptom:* Family members acting badly. They "forget" to invite you and your kid(s) to annual gatherings, freely (and ignorantly) judge your parenting decisions and your kid's behaviors, ask your emotionally impaired kid pointedly hurtful questions—like, "Why can't you be more like your cousin, who's going to Harvard next fall, and has a nice girlfriend too?"

   Solutions:
   - Get real. Tell them exactly how their behavior and comments make you and your family feel.
   - Give them the information they need about your kid's mental illness and the challenges you face as a parent. Email them links or snail-mail them photocopies of articles. Read aloud (without names or other identifying information) what the other parents in your virtual networks are saying—it can help when people see it's not just you. Sometimes it takes a neutral source to convince ignorance to smarten up and mend its ways.

• Some people will never allow themselves to be enlightened. Know when to cut your losses and walk away—even from family. If time spent with parents, siblings, or extended family results in emotional trauma, that is time badly spent. You deserve better than their ongoing emotional assaults.

3. *Symptom:* Your friends have stopped reaching out. They just aren't on your wavelength anymore. Their experiences have been so different than yours—maybe they don't know what to say. Maybe they're afraid they'll hurt you by talking about their own healthy, "normal," family lives. Maybe they find your anxious, depressed demeanor to be depressing and anxiety provoking. This all makes a sad kind of sense, unfortunately—but it doesn't have to mean the death of your friendships. Things have changed, but change is inevitable anyway.

Solutions:
• Let them know you're feeling down about what you perceive as your friendship drifting apart—but try not to sound accusatory.
• Tell them you understand the challenges of maintaining a friendship with someone who's not reliably available anymore, who may be called away abruptly at any moment. Who may not always feel "up" when you want them to.
• Explain why you've become the current you, presuming they don't already know. (If they do know, explain what that all means on a granular level.) Tell them the changes in you are necessity, not choice. (Another way to frame it: you've had to choose between being the best parent you can to your suffering child, and your own social life, but that doesn't mean you don't still treasure your friendships. True friends will hear that, and value it.)
• Ask them not to give up on you. (I often hear myself saying to friends I've not kept actively in touch with, "Thank you for not giving up on me!") If they know in advance that you'll decline more invitations than you'll accept, but that being asked makes you feel good, they may stress less about including you.
• Let them know that even if you appear glum on the rare occasions you're able to see them, you still enjoy their company. If you're not having fun, you'll excuse yourself and go home. And if you sense your blues are bringing them down, you'll work on cheering up—or leave, and ask for a rain check.

SHED 'EM. JUST LET THEM GO:
OUR STORY, SNAPSHOT #13

This is a story of friendship and friend loss, of cultivating and culling a relationship garden.

Like most parents, Lars and I have absorbed both wise and ignorant feedback on our parenting. To parents whose kids are traveling alternative developmental or emotional paths, the standard parenting playbook rarely applies. Unfortunately, the standard human doesn't usually understand this, which means we take a lot of crap from people who don't know what they're talking about.

There's a qualitative difference between well-meaning advice of the "I really think it's a bad idea to let Lucy leave the dinner table and eat in her room" type—even when you take it and things blow up in your face— and plain old mischief making (for example, pulling one of you aside and insinuating that the other is not pulling his weight, or doing this parenting routine all wrong. Yeah, that happens). The former is forgivable, if not very useful. The latter? Nope, not forgivable at all.

Until not so long ago, we had some close, in-the-trenches-with-us friends with bookish credentials and classroom experience in the field of disability, and even hands-on practice, though not, it seems, with maladies of the psyche. Still, we believed their advice to be sterling. We relied upon it to make crucial life decisions, for Benjy, for us as a family—even when we questioned its underlying logic. (Of all the things we questioned, we questioned our own instincts most of all.)

When we acted on their advice, someone would invariably end up more physically ill (me), rehospitalized (Benjy), or more angry and depressed (Lars). Oh, and bitterly divided (Lars and me), especially after spending time with these friends.

They ought to have been able to distinguish illness from malingering. The crippling cost of disability parenting from spendthrift habits. They should have toned down the judgmentalism. Acknowledged their own limits—known how much they didn't know, recognized their biases—before offering us bad counsel.

Of course, they should have done all these things—except they're only people, flawed and myopic like the rest of us. I wouldn't say the unrest they sowed was inadvertent, but I guess it was emotionally complicated on all sides.

Should Lars and I have leaned less on their emotional support? Maintained some skepticism about their expertise, given that the colossal challenges in parenting a suicidal, bipolar, reality-testing child were merely theoretical to them? Were we unrealistic to expect that the reality of a seven-year-old flaying his own skin, restlessly seeking sharp objects, and begging for an escape route out of this world, would transport them to our parallel universe and set them down in our shoes?

Probably so. But we were only human, flawed and myopic like all of humanity.

The truth is, we lived in parallel *and* different universes. Ours was neither more nor less real and true than theirs, just built on alternative scaffolding. I think they couldn't fathom why our lives, our families, and our choices were not carbon copies of theirs. Why we could never seem to save any money, or why only one of us two parents could hold down a paying job.

These people came into my life along with Lars—they'd been his friends first, and then became ours. We loved them. But I suppose they preferred Lars to me, and in a stealthy way began to pit him against me. My rising autoimmunity and connective tissue disease looked to them not like illness but a preference not to "work." (I will just point out here that until my illness erupted so hot I could barely stand on my feet, I *did* work—at the same time working my unpaid gig as triage nurse and wrangler in chief of our considerable family collection of medical and mental health challenges. As time passes, I continue to collect diagnoses like some people collect Hummel figurines.) To them, I looked like a leech and a financial drain. Selfish, extravagant, entitled. There was no illness, no helpless despondency, that could account, in the narrow view of these good friends, for the way we lived.

I'm telling this story, readers, not to vent but because it's an example of relationships poorly tended. A cautionary tale. Too much assumption and not enough communication. Festering resentments. A desperate neediness settling in and clouding our faith in our own abilities.

Lars and I are lucky. The chokehold these friends—better just say "frenemies" and be done with it—had on our relationship finally landed us in couple's therapy. And in that protected space, with the help of a wonderful clinician, we relearned how to communicate with each other and believe in each other. We learned that, in order to preserve *us*—our own challenged, deeply loved family, four persons deep—we had to let those toxic frenemies go.

Maybe as I write this they're wondering about us. Why we never understood them, how it is we caused them nothing but grief. I don't know, and as we've moved on from that rough patch I probably never will.

One day soon after we'd cut them loose, with the hurt still eating at me, I unloaded the whole story on a fellow disability mom. She is a wily, smart, and strong woman, and an honest friend. She told me how to wrest my emotional self free.

"Shed 'em," she said. "Like that hair on your shirt." We were standing—where else?—among the daylilies and foxgloves in my small garden plot. She plucked a fallen strand off the back of my T-shirt and flicked it into the sunshiny air. I saw it rise and shimmer and disappear in the space of a blink. "Just let them go. Life is too hard and short for that kind of crap."

THE MOTHER-LOAD:
MOMS ON MANAGING CHILDHOOD MENTAL
ILLNESS—WITHOUT MUCH HELP FROM DAD

Want to hear what mental health parenting with a partner feels like, straight from the horse's mouth? Scour the web for discussion/support groups for parents of children with emotional impairments, then search the threads using keywords like "relationships." (Most major health and wellness websites, including WebMD.com, Livestrong.com, Drugs.com, Psychcentral .com, to name a few, host mental health–oriented discussions. There are private groups on Facebook too.)

Below, I've stitched together a bunch of posts and comments inspired by real ones found on various online discussion boards. These are faithful to the spirit of the originals, but rewritten by me to shield the identity of the writers and their families. Most of the originals are publicly accessible to anyone with a computer and a search engine. My sample is small, but highly representative of parent experience. This is not to say that dads never step up to the plate; some do, with courage, compassion, and a commitment to helping their kids and partners make it.

Mom 1: After another of my son's meltdowns, where he got super aggressive, I shared one of these posts with my significant other. It was written by a mom, as usual. He said, where are the posts from dads? I really don't remember any posts by men here—are guys even involved much in this? Am I missing something? Mine is ridiculously incapable of dealing with anything my son does. He either escalates the situation or just storms out of the house and comes back after everyone's asleep. He is less than no help. Imagine if we moms just stormed out every time our kids blow up? Haha, that's the day hell freezes over. . . . My husband is clueless how exhausting it is to always be the one dealing with this stuff. I always have to be in the middle of the sh*tstorm, because he has no compassion or understanding. Like, I'm the family referee. He doesn't believe that [our son] can't help it! I try to hold it together, but sometimes I lose it and start screaming back at [my son] too. Not my finest moments . . . I am just so *tired*, you guys . . . trying to fix everything and satisfy everyone and never accomplishing anything because it feels like I am pulled in eight different directions at once. I got my own mental health issues too, but I always end up being the "fixer" no matter how much I'm suffering. And then my husband doesn't understand why I can't "just be happy," which would be convenient for him, but . . . ARE YOU KIDDING ME??? ARGGGHHHH. Sorry for the rant, just seeking a little solidarity here.

Mom 2: I have been divorced for 11 years and my kids rarely see their father (his choice, not ours). My youngest was hospitalized for almost 6 months. Guess what? One email from Dad that whole time. We're near Denver, hospital is an hour drive from my place and about 40 minutes from my ex's. No visits, no phone calls. One email. Half an email, honestly. Breaks my heart but what can you do?

Mom 3: Not all men, though. My husband isn't even my kids' biological father but he's supportive and participates as much as you'd expect. I'm so sorry, Mom 2!! It's really horrible that her dad wasn't there to help support her (and you).

Mom 4: Virtual hugs, Mom 1. Looks like what we get from the dads is never ideal. But we are not getting the ideal either way. My husband's a bit better than what I'm reading here, I know I'm lucky. He will leave work if I call him in a panic (when I can reach him, anyway). He participates in hospital intakes and such. But I don't count on him learning anything about our kids' diagnoses . . . we have 2 with severe anxiety and one of them has bipolar on top of that. I send him links or print out stuff and leave it on his side of the bed (cuz his desk is so cluttered he'd never find it, lol!). Does he read them? Ha! Of course not. But he always has an opinion about what's wrong with the kids and it's usually that they just have to suck it up and knuckle down. I could scream. Still, I know it could be worse. And I actually think he's getting better at this. It seems like the dads have more of a learning curve? Anyway, hang in there, you're not alone!!

Mom 5: My husband just fans the flames when my daughter's melting down. He always does exactly the wrong thing, and leaves me to pick up the pieces. I am so full of resentment! I'd leave, tbh, because I think life would be somewhat easier, but I have no money. We'd be homeless, no joke. I haven't worked since the girls were 4 and 2. It's not like we live like a couple, anyway . . . he's so angry and on edge about the kids, how am

I going to want to have sex with him?? I don't like him right now. He is NOT cut out for being a dad to a bipolar kid, that's for sure. No empathy, no parental instincts.

Mom 6: Hang in there, good mommas! You're all doing everything you can in a truly shitty situation. I love my hubs dearly, but my Lord, when he jumps in things go from really bad to effing HORRIBLE. It would be kinda funny if it weren't killing us. He tries to help, and yes he does mean well. Eventually I just send him out to pick up toilet paper or something. I literally have to pretend we are out of something we need, or tell him I think a box of doughnuts will help calm [our son] down. He tries, but his instincts are laughably (tragically) bad. *Sigh*

Mom 7 (that's *me*!): I can't pass up this opportunity to tell an anecdote of my own. Lars is a wonderful husband and dad. Lars was also an undiagnosed depressed and anxious person for the first 15 years of our marriage. The ongoing traumatic stress in our home only exacerbated his symptoms—and in Lars, those emotions tend to express themselves as anger. Not the best ingredient to toss into an already-boiling domestic stew! I knew he needed treatment (hey, I've been around the block way too many times—diagnosing Lars was easy for me) but was afraid to bring it up. I thought that might spark a metaphorical house fire . . . and it was already hot enough in our home, thank you!

How good of Lars, then, to provide the perfect opening.

It had been a tough morning for us. Lars had lost his keys and his wedding band for the third time that week. Work sucked. He was getting no exercise, and our communication consisted of eye rolls and sarcastic comments (me) and angry outbursts (him). He left for work and I went to the store. His call a few minutes later was no surprise—he often called from work or en route there. But this time his voice stunned me. I knew immediately something was wrong.

"Are you OK?"

"No." He told me, in a dark, almost dissociated voice, he'd been driving 100 mph on Route 95, the highway he took to work. Yes, you heard that right—100 miles per hour. And it wasn't because he's German and imagined, momentarily, he was cruising the Autobahn in a fancy German sports car. (He drives a little tan Toyota Corolla, a perfectly respectable car for anyone's grandma.) The cop who stopped him screamed at him. Humiliated him. And said, "You are gonna be *so poor* after you get this ticket. . . ." We were already strapped, so I imagine those words stung like a swarm of wasps. They sure stung me. But I heard something else in them: leverage.

"OK," I said, doing my best to sound sympathetic (I was actually outraged and bitterly frustrated). "We'll figure this out. I'm not mad at you. But now you owe me. First, never, ever do that again. And second, make an appointment—today—with a psychiatrist. You need mental health treatment. If you won't do it for you, do it for the rest of us. We love you, and we need you alive, not dead."

That driving violation may have been the best thing that ever happened to our family. I handed him a list of names, and he chose one. Getting help with his own psychiatric issues gave Lars the emotional and cognitive space to be a better, more constructively involved parent and life partner.

THIS BLOG MAY GET YOU IN TUNE WITH OTHERS:
JUDITH E. GLASER ON *LISTENING TO CONNECT*

Judith Glaser writes about optimizing communication in the workplace, but her concept of "listening to connect" is widely relevant to personal relationships—and mental health parenting. Consider using her technique to reboot or restore your challenged relationships. In Glaser's own words:

> Listening to Connect is the most powerful catalyst for growth. When we listen to connect, we create space for others to show up, grow up, and become someone new; to have a way to talk about what is really going on inside. When we create space for others to find the words to translate what is going on inside of them at a "chemical level" to find the right words to "share" what they are feeling or thinking about—this is affirming and powerful—finding our voice is vital for health.
>
> Alternatively, when we listen to judge or confirm what we know, we impose on others a label through which we see them and interact with them every day. When we listen to judge, we impose our beliefs about them and shape them into the person we think we are seeing or we want to see—and often we limit their power and potential. They become a diminished version of themselves. When we listen to connect—we allow their aspirational self to emerge—the self that wants to grow. We think out loud with them, co-create with them, and share their dreams with them—that is healthy. Yet we often take away that space with our need to be right.[1]

The Mother-Load, Abridged Version

Moms seem typically more involved than dads in the day-to-day grind of parenting and advocacy, more detail oriented, more educated about their kids' disorders, often resentful of the lack of spousal help, and *exhausted*. Bad news for the health of parental relationships.

Yet: as rough as these situations can get, I still believe that tuning in, finding that point of contact, and transforming *"talking at"* to *"talking with"* can make a big difference in stabilizing and improving the relationships you feel are worth fighting for. (Of course, those *should not ever include unsafe, physically or emotionally abusive ones*, which are imminently dangerous to you and your kids.)

SELECTED RESOURCES FOR
BUILDING BETTER RELATIONSHIPS

Marriage Maintenance

1. Find a good couples therapist/support group/psychiatrist in your area:
   - www.psychologytoday.com
   - https://www.aamft.org (American Association of Marriage & Family Therapists)
   - Whatever Dr. Google turns up—just follow the search strategies from chapter 1, so you don't accidentally diagnose yourself with fatal familial insomnia while researching couples therapy on the web. It happens, trust me.

2. Connect with others dealing with similar issues. (See point 1 above . . . or tap into your parent networks.)

3. Do something that gets your pulse racing (and heart fluttering):
   - Dance! When the kids are absent, or present but safe, put on fast music, slow music, music you can do jumping jacks to, a minuet, a waltz . . . anything, as long as you do it together.
   - If you're two of those alien beings who love exercise, you can do that together too. I'm told it's good for you! Just keep it friendly, people . . . no racing, no technique shaming. Bonus points for laughing your way through the agony (*kidding!*).

4. Yuk it up! Remember that movie where Robin Williams plays a doctor who clowns around with patients at the hospital? (*Patch Adams,*

1998) That guy was right—laughter heals. So, pop some corn, get comfy on the couch with your honey, and chuckle together.

- Stream funny movies/TV. (Remember to scooch close while you watch.)
- Be your own private book club. Set aside time to read the same, agreed-upon book. Read it separately alone, or listen to the audio version of it together. (You could even take turns reading aloud to each other.) Reserve your first twenty minutes in bed for discussing it. (Best to keep your joint reading funny/light when your partnership is flagging.) Highly recommended by yours truly: Anything by Carl Hiaasen, but especially *Sick Puppy* and *Lucky You*. You will laugh your way through them.

Family Functionality

1. Consider family-systems therapy for lessons in refunctionalizing all your dysfunctional family habits. https://www.psychologytoday .com/therapy-types/family-systems-therapy
2. Make equal time for all members of your junior varsity team— a.k.a. the kids! It's hard, I know. The most resources tend to go to the neediest child—as by necessity, they should. But all your kids need to feel they're special to you. Plan something meaningful to do with each of them, separately. If there's no way you can possibly manage it—with the pressures of work, finances, and ongoing mental health crises (yours or anyone else's)—look into Big Brothers Big Sisters (http://www.bbbs.org/), or other mentoring programs for kids.
3. Ask. Listen. Explain. Ask and listen again. Repeat ASAP.

   - Communication is key. Make it age appropriate, try to respect their pushback when they need a break from talk, and don't take it personally when they take out all their anger and frustration on you.
   - If they refuse to communicate verbally with you, draw with them, or listen to music. Even watching a movie or TV show that allows for interactivity can create a space for healing communication. Read how I did just that with my daughter Saskia, in chapter 2, "Making Peace with the TV: Our Story, Snapshot #4."

- If you still can't get them to open up, offer to connect them with a Big Brother or Big Sister, a therapeutic mentor, a sibling support group, or a therapist to whom they can safely vent. They will probably decline. Just keep offering, until they say yes.

Friendship Functionality

1. You don't need a ton of active friendships. It may sound harsh, but your time and energy are limited—and your family and you come first.
2. Think of your friendships as though they were garments in your closet: Which ones are you naturally drawn to, and which feel less comfortable?
3. If a friendship is more dutiful than pleasurable, consider letting it go.
4. There's often a natural waning in friendships that have run their course. Just go with the flow, and don't feel guilty about it. If one less relationship to tend is a relief to you, it probably is to them too.
5. Be alert to the natural rhythms of your friendships. If you only manage to connect with certain friends twice a year, but still care about them—and they care about you—simply accept the rhythm. It will probably change and change again. Nothing wrong with that.
6. If a friendship is mutually valued, but life is too hard for seeing anyone other than family right now, tell them! True friends will have your back, and they'll be there, waiting with open arms, when you're ready to reengage.

"HE BLAMED MY HISTORY OF MENTAL ILLNESS": RENA'S STORY

In chapter 3, I spoke with Rena and Jacob, parents to Jessie and Adam, about the challenges they face parenting two kids, one of whom has autism spectrum and bipolar disorders, the other, anxiety and learning disabilities. Here again, Rena (an amazing mother and a courageous fighter) opens up—this time about the factors that jeopardized her marriage to Jacob, and how the couple managed to pull back together in the end.

Rena: It was always my dream to have that perfect family: a husband, two kids, a couple of dogs, and a little house with a white picket fence. Corny, I know. But that's the family I never had.

My parents are both mentally ill. Both narcissists. And they were always so caught up in their self-centered dramas, I was essentially an abandoned child.

I promised myself I would be the best, most loving, most nurturing mom ever, if I was lucky enough to have a family of my own . . . because I know what it's like when you get the opposite. It's awful.

No great surprise that I have my own mental health issues . . . depression and anxiety, mostly. When Jacob and I had our first baby (who we later found out had a mood disorder, Asperger's syndrome, and anxiety) she was tough. Always irritable and oppositional. We endured a ton of stress from the get-go . . . but she was our first, beautiful baby, and we had nothing to compare her to. We just thought, *Oh, OK, this is parenting.*

The problem was not that we didn't love her and fight every day for her to have a little happiness and well-being. It was that the ongoing stress began to bite into *our* mental health and well-being. And we didn't know how to communicate about it. It can be easier to just keep your head down and push on, you know? Easier in the short run. *Not* better.

It's a long story, but one day, I snapped. Jacob and I had been on edge for a long time. Not connecting, squabbling over everything. My anxiety and depression had gotten to the point where I felt everyone would be better without me in the picture. I knew that Jacob thought our older child's problems were my fault, that I was exacerbating her breakdowns with my responses to them. He'd decided I was crazy, like my parents. Really. If you ask him even today, he will tell you I tend to spiral with the kids rather than pulling them back up. At that time, ten years ago, I believed him. I had to be crazy, I was born to be crazy. My self-esteem was so low—less than zero. The worse things got with us, the more I felt blamed by Jacob. His parents live in a nearby town, and they sided with him, of course. (Mine were, and are, MIA, which is probably all for the best.)

The day I downed a bottle or two of pills was after Jacob took the kids from me and went with them to live at his parents' house. I felt I had lost everything. I was so alone. Everyone knew I was mentally ill. I was obviously a bad mother . . . hurting my own children. I'd really believed I could do this parenting thing right, I could outwit my genes and be the parent I never had. And my own husband showed me how mistaken I'd been. I was sure the kids hated me. I was ready to go.

There's a blacked-out period after I took those pills, but I did end up in the hospital for weeks, and our family was referred to the Department of Children and Families [DCF]. That was the most humiliating thing in my life so far: having my parenting scrutinized by some twenty-five-year-old kid from DCF, fresh out of grad school, who'd hardly even lived yet.

There's nothing to prepare you for something like this, right? That life with a husband and two beautiful kids and a house and a couple of dogs could be so cruel.

Well. I'm sitting here with you, which obviously tells you I failed my own suicide. That's one failure I'm happy about. Life has gotten better in small increments—and sometimes we backslide, which I suppose is normal—but whatever comes, I am going to be fully present for all of it.

Nothing is exactly easy, even now . . . we are fighting mental illness every day, one day at a time. On the plus side: Jacob and I have rebuilt our trust. He's great about participating in our daughter's mental health treatment and education. I don't know many dads who get in there like he does. He is willing to listen and learn, and I'm grateful for that.

I would give my kids the world if I could. I wish I could just take all their burdens on my own back.

"I HAVE TO GIVE HIM SPACE TO FEEL HIS PAIN": LENA'S STORY

I spoke via Skype with Lena, an entrepreneur and mom to four, living with her husband and kids in Paris. Her second child, Andre, is fifteen years old and severely affected by complex mental illnesses. The family also includes two younger children, both girls, and an adult older brother who lives on his own.

Lena: We are American expats living in France. In some ways the mental health care system is better here—especially in the way they consider the well-being of the whole family when your kid needs mental health services. My second boy, Andre, is a teenager and has all kinds of issues . . . he is on the autism spectrum, bipolar, let's see . . . he has oppositional defiant disorder, and he's just angry—all the time. I have never known him except as a rageful person.

Andre's always expressed his feelings in destructive ways: anger, aggression, antisocial behaviors, shoplifting, things like that. You really don't ever see sadness or joy or even fear in him. And as he gets bigger and stronger, being with him gets scarier.

He's been in and out of hospitals and institutions here in Paris. He's been arrested for stealing, more than once. Sometimes it feels like all I do is clean up after him, trying to deal with social workers, family court, and everyone else who's involved in his case, in my schoolgirl French (my husband never even tried to learn the language). Basically, I cross my fingers and hope for the best.

Sometimes it's hard to love Andre, because he doesn't appear to love back. That's so horrible for a mother to say, right? Well, I'm not proud of it, but what can I do? *Jesus*, look what's become of us! I am so depleted from living this way. I'm so tired. I feel helpless, you know? Like we're just sitting here and waiting for the next earthquake to strike, no place to run, and this time it might actually destroy us.

Andre is not OK, my marriage is not OK, my youngest two, his little sisters, are not OK living under this cloud. I wish someone would tell me how a family is supposed to live like this! The sad thing is, I don't think it would be better back in the States. Not in the Southeast, where we come from. Anyway, we've cast our lot here, and we're not turning back.

Oh—but something new did happen recently. Andre's in the hospital, waiting for a spot in yet another residential school to open up for him. He's not getting any treatment, mind you, just killing time in the locked unit till he can go be someone else's "burden." It's not safe to have him here at home anymore. (Long pause, deep breath.) That's sad, no? But I've been dealing with it. I finally managed to put up an emotional barrier; I convinced myself it was OK to step back and focus on my other kids, my marriage, myself.

So anyway, it's almost Christmas and Andre is not coming home. I called him, I'm not sure why because I wasn't going to, and we talked and he cried and cried. Real tears. Not manipulative, not angry tears, but despondent. He's fifteen and alone at Christmas.

But look, I see this as progress—he's allowed himself to feel an emotion he's spent his whole life fighting against. Maybe there's a chance for him yet. I know he can't help his behaviors; I know he's ill. But I'm trying to come to terms with the fact that I've done all that I can for my son, and now I've got to give him the space he needs to feel his own pain, and to grow into it.

AS ONE ASCENDED, THE OTHER SLID: JANICE'S STORY

Janice lives on the West Coast, and is a community college professor, wife, and mother to two sons. I asked her about the way childhood psychiatric disorder has affected her family. She spoke mainly on the sibling factor, describing what turns out to be a common phenomenon in families of kids with mental health disorders: they take turns!

Janice: My sons are two years apart. The oldest, James, had a pretty rough start in life. Delayed motor development, speech impairments, social awkwardness, general immaturity . . . He was super bright but struggled with some basic things you sort of assume every kid just knows how to do (reading social cues, for example). His hyperliteral take on things—it was all black and white with James, no nuance—made friendships hard. It caused problems at home too. For whatever reason, his younger brother, Henry, was this huge trigger: all Henry had to do was walk into the room and James would flip out. You couldn't reason with him when it came to his brother. Their relationship was a zero-sum game—it was James or Henry, in James's mind. So, every encounter between them was like World War 3, 4, 5. . . .

James was a lot louder than Henry, and much more obvious with his issues. By the age of what, twelve? maybe thirteen? he was having meltdowns bad enough that we had to take him to the ER, and he was admitted a few times to inpatient psych. I can imagine—well, I *know*, but only after the fact—how hard it was for Henry. He felt responsible for his brother's problems, because he was the obvious trigger. So, when my husband and I decided to send James to a boarding school that would do a better job with his needs than our public schools were doing, Henry took it hard. And here's what gets me: my husband and I could *not* see that.

He was making straight As in school. He was an athlete—soccer and baseball. But secretly, inside, he was decompensating. So, as James got emotionally healthier, away at school, Henry was developing some serious mental health problems.

Yeah, as one ascended, I guess, the other one slipped.

I could go on forever about it, because this is one giant puzzle of a story and I still haven't sorted out all the pieces. But Henry experienced a couple of deep depressions early in high school, which my husband and I didn't really view as serious at the time. He just presented differently than his brother, you know? On top of everything else, he injured his knee and could no longer do sports. That was a real blow, because his identity was so wrapped up in athletics.

And then he started gambling—at the poker table, online, anywhere he could. We were blindsided by it.

Since then, it's been really touch and go with Henry. He's siphoned money from my bank account to feed the addiction, been in and out of the hospital, dropped out of school, gotten his hands on his own credit cards and created a huge financial mess for himself—after making one for his dad and me.

Henry was always quieter than his brother, harder to read. He was the kind of kid who could pass for "normal"—healthy, I should probably say—if he had to. I wonder sometimes whether he felt he *had* to pass, because he saw that his dad and I were up to our ears in his brother's drama—and he felt responsible, poor kid.

You can only tamp that stuff down for so long, whatever it is—anxiety, depression, panic, a tic. Things bubble up. So yeah. The kid we thought we didn't need to worry about is the one who's struggling the most after all. They took turns with their mental health issues. I have no idea how this all turns out . . . we've learned not to overfocus on the future.

THE TAKEAWAY

1. Choose your relationships carefully. Quality trumps quantity when it comes to the people you spend time with.
2. Learn which friendships and family relationships to "shed." You don't need any extra toxicity in your life.
3. Good communication is the key to every fulfilling relationship—with partner, kids, relatives, and friends.

   - Tune in.
   - Find your point of contact.
   - Engage, to transform "talking at" to "talking with."

4. Know the symptoms of—and solutions to—"relationship breakdown," including:

   - Loss of emotional and physical intimacy with your partner

     ○ Talk about it.
     ○ Listen respectfully to your partner's side.
     ○ Ask what your partner needs to feel cared for; indicate what you need.
     ○ Engage in affectionate touch, positive mutual attention, and laughter.
     ○ Invest in couple's therapy.

   - When friends and family make insensitive comments, and/or "disinvite" you to gatherings

     ○ Pipe up about the issues you're dealing with.
     ○ Use it as a "teaching moment." Inform them about your kid's disabilities and the resultant family dynamic.

- ° Tell them how being left out and/or misunderstood makes you feel, without putting them on the defensive.
- ° If need be, just let go. (Feel free to indulge in all the name-calling and ranting you want, but try to do so privately. Burning bridges, though we all do it, is bad policy in general.)

Ultimately, good communication is a form of self-care, as well as a method for parenting and partnering well. Learn how to do it, and keep practicing!

OPEN MIC: KIDS SPEAK OUT

Brydget, Age Seventeen, California

When I'm depressed, the thing I need most is space. I need my mom to *not* get in my face about what's wrong. She thinks asking me if I'm OK, if I want to talk, if something bad happened at school, blah blah blah is gonna make me not depressed anymore. Like she could just step in and fix it, if I'd only tell her about my life. She's a sweet lady and a good mother, but she can be clueless.

It's hard for me to tell my mom what I need, because I'm afraid I'll hurt her feelings. I appreciate that she only wants to help . . . she just has no idea how my brain works, and I really can't explain that to her. I guess she never noticed that if she leaves me alone for a few hours, I come out of my room feeling better.

What *does* help me get out of a depression, is I take some alone time and maybe watch some inspiring YouTube videos or draw some cartoons. Also I think about my friends and the fact that I'm not an outcast like I used to be. My friends are really great. They care about me and respect who I am as a person.

6

THE KEY TO BETTER ACCESS
AND CARE MAY BE AT
THE TIP OF YOUR TONGUE

The mental health system in our country is failing vulnerable children—my kids, your kids, and statistically speaking, millions of others.

The problem isn't necessarily a lack of talented and determined mental health care providers among us. I'm willing to bet that the U.S. boasts some of the very best clinicians and researchers in the world. Ditto for good intentions. In theory, and excepting the inevitable bad apples, our health care systems and providers *want* to help kids—and people of all ages.

But, just as we see in our public education system—the two intersect, for obvious reasons—good people and sterling intentions don't always translate to ethical treatment or positive outcomes. The problem is multilayered, and exacerbated by

- the constraints imposed by the outlandish cost of health care in this country;
- a cultural resistance to seeing mental illnesses as "real" disorders rather than bad behavior and poor choices; and
- the challenges inherent in diagnosing and treating disorders of the psyche.

These barriers to affordable, accessible, and fair mental health resources, like the other hurdles taken on in this book, are formidable but not insurmountable. If you put on your rose-colored glasses and view them from a different angle, you can accept these hurdles as a challenge to become your child's most effective advocate—and maybe kick the system's butt while you're at it. (If you're weeping with despair after reading this, it's quite all right—I've been weeping on and off for years. You can always try to kick some butt another day.)

FIVE THINGS I WISH I KNEW FROM THE BEGINNING

1. Entering our mental health care system is like visiting a foreign country. Learning the language and customs is harder than you thought it would be—but now that you live there, you'll slowly catch on.
2. You *must be a partner* in your own and your family's health care. Without your vigilance, proactivity, and follow-through, things will always go worse than you'd hoped they would. Why? No one cares about your child's health like you do—and to health care providers, every patient is just one blade of grass in a meadow.
3. You will never be a partner in your kid's care unless you believe you *can* and *should* be one . . . and then learn how to communicate effectively with his providers.
4. Childhood mental health clinicians are as prone to trauma as you are. After all, they see what you see, and then some, every day at their job. It's not the same as watching your own child suffer, 24/7, but it may explain the protective shield many erect when you enter their orbit.
5. Practice empathy toward the gatekeepers and providers of care, and tacitly encourage them to practice it back at you. Your odds of helping your child increase vastly when the folks with the years of training and Rx pads are fully invested in the outcome.

CHILDHOOD MENTAL ILLNESS
AND THE MIGHTY BOTTOM LINE

It can't buy you love. It can't buy you happiness. But money sure does make the world go around. Those of us struggling to obtain decent mental health care, or therapeutic education services for kids, are reminded of this lousy truth every day. If, as special education advocate Cynthia Moore argued in chapter 4, money drives every decision about disability services in American public education, the same can certainly be said for mental health care in our country, which is typically less available, and more costly to patients (in terms of finances and outcomes), than physical medical care.

It's *hard* to find the right services and treatment options for our kids! Half the time we have no idea what we're supposed to do, or even what we're looking for. And when we finally figure it out, we often face a bruising fight with our insurance providers—or a hospital bed waiting list so long that we just crawl home and pray our kids survive the wait.

The bottom line is: it's largely about the bottom line. What kind of insurance coverage you have (if any), the quality of the facilities where your child gets treatment, and whether you can access prescription medications and regular mental health care all depend on the profit and loss calculus.

Most families confronting a serious childhood illness—of *any* kind—end up financially strapped and emotionally zapped by the experience. This bottom line of the bottom line is a rather big problem.

FAKE, OR REAL?

As if the money-buys-you-access issue weren't enough, stigma and disinformation are alive and well, thank you very much—even, sadly, among the ranks of our mental health and social services workers. You could be as certain as humanly possible that your son's rages are not just "something he'll outgrow" or the result of overindulgent parenting. You might still end up searching far and wide for a clinician who will take you seriously, venture a diagnosis, or confirm the last professional's diagnosis, rather than snarkily cutting it down. You could sob abjectly at the feet of the umpteenth social worker who tells you, "We don't really *have* any programs for children like your daughter. I'm not sure who does. . . . " and you know what? Your experience would not be unusual.

The forgivable explanation for this is that the human psyche is opaque and confounding to begin with; when it goes off kilter, there is no unambiguous route to diagnosis, or set-in-stone treatment protocol. Even the best-informed, open-minded providers may struggle to find reasonable answers, or take a long time going about it.

> What the world does not yet know about the human brain could probably fill an entire universe.

One unforgivable but common explanation for the troubles we encounter when seeking diagnosis and treatment for our kids and help for our families, is that young people with emotional disorders are viewed by a significant portion of the public as bad kids—undisciplined at home, poorly parented, or inherently broken. Why waste your time on people like that? Why waste precious resources on kids who don't want to be good, when little babies are dying of cancer, every day?

It's pretty clear where opinions like this come from—or why providing quality, affordable treatment for our kids ends up low on our national to-do list. But we don't have to accept this status quo without a fight! Childhood cancer is an unspeakable tragedy. So is a life-threatening, pediatric mental illness. Why should our kids be subject to a moral comparison, when illness simply is not a moral issue? You know, and I know, that a bodily disease has no more "legitimacy" than a psychiatric one—even if large numbers of our fellow Americans haven't gotten that message yet.

I'm not the first to say this and I won't be the last, but maybe our best hope for healing and protecting kids like ours will be to *change the cultural narrative on mental illness.* It can't be done in a day, readers. Maybe not even in our own lifetimes. It's a big, complicated, overwhelming job. I'm not really sure what it entails, beyond a commitment, by those of us who *can* speak publicly about mental health and illness, to speaking loud and often and true.

But what if there were something we could do, right now, that might topple some of these barriers to good mental health care for our kids? Money. Stigma. Access. The inscrutability of the psyche.

Remember, we are a potentially mighty army. I think we can take down those barriers, if just partially, using peaceful but firm tactics: situational intelligence, smart communication, and a double dose of determination.

EXCUSE ME—ARE WE
SPEAKING THE SAME LANGUAGE?

You might have entered the world of mental health parenting with some determination to get important stuff done, in collaboration with the people who doctor, teach, or offer therapeutic services to your kid. (Or at least, with the idea that you would get the experts the facts they need, so they could do their thing and start helping your child.) And why wouldn't you approach it that way? Chances are, you and your child's providers all speak and understand English, even if yours or theirs is accented, marble mouthed, or less than fluent. This talking-and-listening skill is one you probably mastered, to some degree, long before your immersion in the world and words of mental illness.

You've got what it takes to scribble down the words you don't know and look them up later—right?

Well . . . in a perfect world, sure—you've got what it takes. In that perfect world, you'd expect the expert to

- speak clearly;
- watch your face and body language for signs you don't understand what he or she is getting at;
- recognize when you need a bit of hand-holding, are feeling stressed, or insulted, or like you might vomit; and
- respond accordingly.

Also in that perfect world, you and I would

- say what we mean and mean what we say;
- leave ambiguity, resentment, and passive-aggressive behavior outside the clinical space;
- drop the self-delusional belief that, even though we haven't understood a single word, or we disagree with everything the doctor just said, we'll pretend otherwise (to preserve our dignity) and deal with it later;
- not bring printed or scrawled lists of questions and concerns and then forget to remove them from our pockets, effectively wasting thirty to sixty "clinical-minutes" (translation: extremely pricey, and over before you know it);
- refuse to feel ashamed that we have to ask for explanations; and
- have the courage to ask, even when the important doctor, busy teacher, or therapist with the next patient waiting outside is glancing at his watch.

> In a perfect world, everyone's interest is aligned, and the beneficiary is the child.

It's a bummer that we don't inhabit that perfect world. In *ours* (which, as I'm sure you know, is highly imperfect), unspoken assumptions, unwritten rules, and dueling agendas make communicating with the experts who wield power over our lives tricky at best. Neither we nor they are adept at hearing words not actually spoken, for one thing—yet between us, so much is left unsaid when we meet with the gatekeepers and providers of our children's health care and education.

For example, no school district—or insurer—is going to *tell* you their primary concern is the Mighty Bottom Line. Instead they'll attribute denial of services to "lack of need," and hope you don't pursue it any further.

You *can't* pursue it if you don't know how to interpret "lack of need" in context. (Ignorance and stinginess are no excuse to ruin a kid's life, but that doesn't mean ignorance and stinginess aren't gonna try.)

Likewise, no clinician who thinks you're a hot mess—chronically late to appointments, forgetful, overly needy, or approval seeking—will openly admit it, nor will they tell you you're getting on their last nerve, until that nerve has snapped. When they start avoiding eye contact, barking short, exasperated answers to your questions, and rushing you out the door with your weeping teenager, you'll finally figure out they're breaking up with you—or pushing you to break up with them. At least, that's what happened to my kid and me.

Here's what my kid's psychiatrist didn't do: look at me and intuit that I'd not slept well for nearly a decade; remember what I told him about the years I'd spent on suicide watch, fretting about financial doom, and dealing with a second child's (milder) anxiety and depression, while trying to juggle too many other balls. Neither did he forgive me for having a PhD and appearing the part, while acting like a person with cognitive impairments. (I will admit to all three of those, the cognitive impairments being a legacy of traumatic stress, poor diet, and exhaustion.)

And here's what *I* didn't do: imagine what it's like to have to repeat the same damned information, time after time, to someone who really ought to have mastered it by now (maybe it seemed to him I wasn't paying attention or taking him seriously); intuit the frustration he must have felt showing up to our appointment, only to hear we weren't going to make it (he could have offered that slot to someone else who needed it, given only a bit more notice); or consider that he is only human. (Could his personal life be in ruins? Maybe *his* kids are falling apart, or he's behind on his mortgage payments.)

Things I wish I'd said to this guy, firmly and without fear, anytime they needed to be said:

- Doctor, I'm sorry we've forgotten what you advised last time about tapering off the Prozac and trying something new. My own cognitive issues are always worse when family members are in crisis, which happens a lot. Can you explain again what you think is the best action?
- I know I am not your patient and not your responsibility, but in order to ensure my child gets the care she deserves, would you either write me a brief note on medication decisions after each visit, or permit me to record your words, so she and I can refer to them if we forget or feel confused?

- I owe you an apology for sometimes canceling appointments on the same day. I am handling all my kids' medical and mental health needs solo, while my husband works long days to keep us afloat. As you know, I am also chronically ill. Living like we do can make us unreliable. Please let me know if this becomes a problem for you, so we can work on a way to resolve it.
- The reason we've been letting months slip by before scheduling follow-ups? It's usually related to having $13.60 in our checking account, and six days till payday. I can't afford the $40 copayment!

Things I wish he'd said to me:

- It looks like life is challenging for you right now. How can I help?
- Here's some information on programs and services you might want to look into for your daughter and yourself.
- I'm sensing these sessions may not be helpful to your daughter or you. Do you think you'd be more comfortable with a woman clinician?
- Would checking in less frequently be a better solution for you? Or vice versa?
- I can only imagine how overwhelmed you must be feeling. You know, things do generally get better. Hang in there, you're not alone!

Wow. Just think of the problem-solving and productive-communication skills we'd have modeled, between us, for the kid in the room, if we'd been able to get that right.

I don't know what the clinician's excuse was—take your pick from my speculative list, above—but my excuse was simply, *this is my life right now*. And I'm ready to forgive myself. I forgive him too, though I doubt we'll cross paths again. Who knows whether he's given us half a moment's thought, since he barked us out of the office that day.

Let's face it: no one's at their best when their child's in psychiatric crisis. Any provider who judges you on how yellow your teeth are, or how enormous your eye bags appear versus your last visit—let alone your own emotional health under the circumstances—is probably not worth the fifty cents you just fed the meter. Not to mention your copayment, coinsurance, deductible, or self-payment. Even if you're on Medicaid and your kid sees his providers free of cost to you, the doctor who makes rude comments about the food stains on Junior's pants, or your frantically donned, inside-out blouse (yep, another true story from the family archives), may not be worth the time spent commuting to see him. Same goes for any kind of professional who works with your child and your family: they add value to your life only when they treat kids and their families with dignity and compassion.

We deal with enough indignities in our lives without our providers spooning out a little more!

> All health care providers must offer the minimum of *asking the right questions and listening to the answers with both one's mind and with one's heart*. Even if we have nothing more, that is the least we must do and some would argue, the most important of all.—Leon Hammer, MD[1]

Now, I know that managing these relationships is harder than I make it sound here. Many of us were raised to treat physicians and other health care providers with deference. We may feel unintelligent or at a loss for words around them. And some doctors can act as though our deference is their entitlement. Don't fall for that! You're the one fighting for your child's health and welfare, perhaps her very life. That's nothing short of heroic. Try not to let anyone make you feel otherwise . . . the mental health work you do for your child is as specialized and as remarkable, in its way, as anything the most credentialed psychiatrist will do for her.

THE SECRET LIVES OF PATIENTS
AND CLINICIANS, PART 1

Have you ever wondered about the inner lives of your health care providers? Do you think they wonder about ours? The medical blog *KevinMD* (www.kevinmd.com) may offer some answers. Poke around there and see what you find; it's an informative browse, if you've got the mental space to read anything other than hospital discharge summaries or beachy novels. I found an answer there to something I've been pondering: What would our kids' providers think if they had access to our private, online parent networks? (1) Would they see in us the warriors for our kids, the bravest of (imperfect) heroes, that we see in each other? (2) Would they think we're ignorant? And (3) would they find, inside our off-kilter corner of the universe, a portal to introspection? (1) Probably. (2) Um . . . yeah, that too. And (3) it looks that way!

In a blog post titled "A Physician Lurked on Facebook Mom Groups. Here's What She Found," a neurologist/mom encounters exactly the clash of cultures you'd expect when she drops in on a Facebook mommy group.

Spoiler alert: Moms would rather seek medical advice from strangers on internet groups than from physicians. (Of course we would! Obviously.)

The writer asks, "Why is it, that despite our best efforts, we are failing our patients? [Why do] they feel so alienated by us that they run to an anonymous internet forum for urgent medical advice[?]" She sees, in the moment, a lesson: there exists an "often-invisible gap of understanding" between doctors and patients—and part of her responsibility to her patients is to try to bridge that gap.[2]

I was so happy to stumble upon this blog post! It gives me real hope that we, on our side of the childhood mental health arena, are not alone in sensing that something is not right with the status quo—and that we can do better.

The bottom line is, *clinicians and patients don't always interact effectively with each other.* The consequences of our mutual miscommunications, misunderstandings, mistrust, and missed opportunities can range from minor inconvenience all the way to catastrophe.

"Situational Intelligence": You've Got It, So Start Using It

Think of the neurologist/mom who peeks inside the parent experience and has an epiphany about the doctor/patient "understanding gap." That is an example of situational intelligence. So is your reaction when you receive an email announcing you've won the Nigerian State Lottery, and you roll your eyes and click Delete. You look at the Nigerian windfall situation in context: the odd grammar, syntax, and salutation conventions in the email itself; the bizarre mismatch between the writer's signature and the email address of sender; the fact that *you've never entered a Nigerian lottery—why would you*; and your knowledge that Nigerian email scams are a thing, out there in the murky interwebs.

I'm not talking about IQ here. Situational intelligence refers to the skills most of us really do have at the ready: alertness to the present situation, life experience/historical awareness, attention to what's being said and how it's conveyed. "Insight" and "perspective" are other words to describe situational savvy.

Try always to be intelligent parent-consumers of mental health services: hyperalert to stigma, disinformation, and distrust in your dealings with the gatekeepers and professionals who parcel out services (those counterproductive forces can lurk inside of them *and* you). Look out for the unspoken messages that can be tucked between the lines of things that are written or said to you. Even if you've been putting out too many fires to bone up on facts and details before discussing what you need with the gatekeepers, you can learn when and how to push back, when to call it a day and return with reinforcements at a different time—simply by watching for unspoken signs, reading and hearing between the lines, and reacting intelligently in the context of that moment.

1. READ BETWEEN THE LINES

- Example: Gatekeeper at a state agency for folks with mental health disorders says, "Oh, no. We don't *provide* the service you're asking about."
  - Parent thought bubble: *She may really be saying, "Budget shortfall!"*
  - Alternative parent thought bubble: *I think she's actually saying, "I have no idea, so I'm gonna say no."*
- Example: Special education director says, "If we're considering a change of placement for a student, we start slow and try all the less extreme options first. So, we would never just refer your child to a private, therapeutic residential school—or even a day school—without at least trying to keep her close to home and with typical peers."
  - Parent thought bubble: *Uh-oh, is he really saying, "I don't think this family knows their rights. Unless the kid starts cutting in the bathroom between classes, I'm not screwing with the budget"?*
  - Alternative parent thought bubble: *Maybe I'm hearing, "Uh, I'm not too sure about the legal implication here, so let's deflect until I can scrounge together the time to figure it out."* [Readers: that thud you just heard was *let's deflect till I figure out if we can legally deny what parents are asking for* falling off SPED director's to-do list.]

2. CHANGE THE CONVERSATION

If you've already done some research, or at least asked around your parent networks and know that some people have indeed received those services through that agency, you can change the conversation. If you don't have the fight (or finesse!) in you at that moment, ask a friend, a fellow mental health parent, an advocate, or your go-to "good cop" or "bad cop" to help you with that conversation. Just make sure you have the information you'll need to start engaging with the gatekeepers and providers of services on a different (and more productive) level.

- Firmly and respectfully show them you've done your research.
  - "Maybe I'm being unclear—I have a bad habit of doing that! I am aware that your agency provides services X and Y, because several parents I consult with on a regular basis have received them from you. Can you help me figure out how to apply for them?"
  - "May I speak with your supervisor? That way, I can just close the book on this issue. I know you guys are busy there, and I don't want to keep calling back and bugging you."
  - "Thanks for your time! Would you please give me the name and number of your agency head, so I can clarify how to access services X and Y, which she described in a speech I recently watched on YouTube?"

Use the same strategy for negotiating with special education administrators:

  - "Well, I've done some scouting online, and I see that our school district has placed a few students in therapeutic, residential schools in the past six years. It turns out a couple of those families are in my network. Why don't I check in with them to see how their process worked, and get back to you?"

It's imperative to be friendly and polite, even when you're demonstrating steely resolve. Don't give anyone an excuse to screw with you or write you off. Just keep calm, know what you're up against, and believe in yourself—no one out there can quite fill your shoes.

The Most Intelligent Communication Strategy Just Might Be Called "Empathy"

If we really want to improve our relationships with the gatekeepers and providers of our kids' mental health care, we'd better work at understanding where *they're* coming from, and at allowing ourselves to be clearly understood. Empathy can help with those endeavors.

Granted, your responsibility ends with you . . . you can't force anyone into your shoes. But there may be ways to gently invite them in for a try-on. For example: if you can read "between the lines" that Dr. Too Busy is feeling peeved by your chronic breathlessness and forgetfulness, or is unwilling to take your concerns about your child as anything other than your own hysteria, you can look for ways to help him find some empathy, by figuring out (generally) what's going on inside of him and responding to it. And you can do it with confidence that you, as your child's front-line first responder, triage nurse, and therapist, are as deserving to be heard, and taken seriously, as he is.

That's what I tried to do when I revisited (on paper) my relationship with my daughter's psychiatrist, earlier in this chapter. I reflected on what was left unspoken on either side and imagined what it would have taken (had Saskia and I felt it worth the effort) to straighten things out by communicating more effectively. In real time, I never thought to ask myself, *Can this relationship be saved?* I tend to be more of a flincher from, than facer of, conflict. There were plenty of shrinks in our neck of the woods—Boston, what can I say?—and enough of them took our insurance that we could cut loose from this guy and find someone kinder. Still, what I proved to myself, if only on paper, is that I could have done things differently if I'd needed to—if, say, he was the only clinician in a twenty-five-mile radius who took our insurance. I could have tried harder to fix all that toxic misunderstanding between us, before giving up. In a way, I wish I had. Those are skills worth practicing and honing, because parents like me will inevitably need to use them, off and on, over our parenting lifetimes.

REBEKAH'S COMMUNICATION NIGHTMARE:
A CAUTIONARY TALE

Rebekah, an occupational therapist in the Pacific Northwest, told me a story involving her daughter that made my blood run cold. It's about a mom and dad advocating desperately with their school district and others on behalf of Gracie, who struggled with anxiety, ADHD, slow processing, and eventually, school-refusal. The parents, who live with Gracie and her two siblings in a desirable suburb of a major city, had yet to learn to read between the lines of what school officials were telling them. They had not yet become the skeptics parents of kids with disabilities must be. And they were still figuring out their own, best communicative approach to the professionals who had so much power over their daughter's well-being—but an agenda misaligned with the family's. Sometimes, as appears to be the case here, it's virtually impossible to bring parties into agreement—and by the time a parent realizes it's going to take a costly, painful, legal action to achieve (with luck) a realignment to the child's interests, all kinds of damage has been done. Unfortunately, lessons like these are hard won . . . and the consequences for families like Rebekah's can be crushing.

Rebekah: I can hardly tell this story without breaking down. You know, we almost lost custody of our daughter last year. Yeah, just in case you thought it was only addicted or neglectful or abusive parents who had their kids taken from them. Our whole family was traumatized and ripped open by this . . . by these people, who were just so ill informed about how to teach kids with emotional or learning issues, and how to relate to those kids' parents! It was a nightmare.

Gracie was always a superbright and creative kid, but I knew from the outset she had a different learning style. Like, you'd give her a multiple-choice question with four possible answers, and in her mind the answer wasn't listed—she'd say, "None of those are right, it's more complicated than that, and here's why." I knew she was going to have trouble in a conventional public school . . . but we'd moved to a suburb with a supposedly awesome school district, and we'd paid a premium for the privilege. I had faith they'd work with Gracie—or with me and my husband—to help manage her learning differences. We just assumed that's what public schools do. I think the fact that, up to the fifth grade, she was mostly happy and successful in school may have blinded the school staff to any problems.

Although the elementary years were fairly smooth sailing, Grace did display what we thought was anxiety. In kindergarten, where she had terrible separation anxiety, my husband would drop her off and she'd just fall apart . . . one time, another parent found her wandering in the parking lot looking for her dad, minutes after she was dropped in the classroom. No one had even noticed—but guess who they blamed when we approached them to ask what had gone wrong? Us!

Here's an example of how inflexible they were at school: Given the separation anxiety, I asked this kindergarten teacher, "Could you maybe greet Gracie at the classroom door when she's dropped off, and give her a special job to do? I think the distraction would help." This is not rocket science, by the way—I'm not an early-childhood educator, but it seems obvious and reasonable to me. She said no, she could not. Mind you, there were two adults in that classroom, and as far as we could tell, only one child—ours—breaking down at drop-off.

That was a huge disappointment—we really didn't understand the teacher's pushback—but we figured it'd get better if we just kept advocating for our child.

Certain other aspects of her experience through elementary school convinced us Gracie had anxiety, as well as attentional issues, but when we brought it up with the school they disagreed. "How could she be doing so well if she has all those issues? There's no problem here."

Well, I guess we didn't fully agree with their rosy assessment.

We had begun asking about special education services in first grade, because that's when Gracie's teacher pointed out she was having trouble getting started on assignments. Just as they would be later, the district was dismissive of our concerns. We asked them at least to evaluate her. They insisted she was just fine, but agreed to do cognitive and emotional/behavioral testing.

The cognitive testing showed that Gracie had severely impaired processing speed. But she scored high in all other areas of cognitive function.

"She's brilliant!" the school district said. "We've never seen scores like that before!" Well, yes—we knew she was smart. We were also worried by the seventy-point gap between her processing speed and her higher-level cognitive skills. That might explain the slow task initiation in the classroom and the growing homework resistance we saw at home. The district brushed it off. Again.

As far as the emotional/behavioral testing went, they saw nothing of note. *Nope, nothing to see here.* They told us what the problem was. Get this: it was our *parenting.* Shocking, right? It was *our* fault.

Oh my God, we were so devastated! But we still trusted the school district, because its reputation was sterling—among the best. And we thought, *What if they're right? Maybe the problem* is *us!* Meanwhile, getting her to do her homework became harder and harder. We fought with her about it every day. It made life at home so stressful—and that wasn't good for any of us. We asked her teachers for help managing the situation—impose some *consequences*, if nothing else!—but they never stepped up.

When Gracie reached sixth grade, my husband and I made a decision: if the school was going to blame the home environment for Gracie's homework refusal, then we would just let the homework go. I think you could safely say we are success-oriented people, so it took a while for us to get there, but if we were contributing to our daughter's stress, then we had to reevaluate. Whether or not the teachers were going to do what they were paid to do and educate her, we had to preserve our relationship with our child and maintain a safe, loving, angst-free space for her at home.

That year, things worked out OK. We stopped bugging Grace and she mostly did the work on her own. It was a few months into seventh grade when the shit really hit the fan.

In our town, transitioning to seventh grade means a school change. We'd met with Gracie's teachers early that year to discuss our hands-off approach to homework, as well as our concerns about her various school-related issues. They told us not to worry—she was doing fine. We requested they notify us if anything changed.

Hmm. Two months later, we heard from the school she was getting Cs and Ds in her classes. If they'd counted the undone homework, she'd be failing half of them. Whatever had happened in those two months, no one bothered to let us know—even though we'd alerted them to the problems and asked them to keep us in the loop!

Well, not long after that, Gracie started refusing to go to school. She'd been told she'd face consequences for not handing in her work, and I guess that was her tipping point. She was done. When we did get her to go to school, she declined to participate. She was rude. We'd never seen anything like this from her. Never! The closest was when she'd refused to take a standardized test the previous year, just never opened the test booklet and never answered a single question. If there's not some underlying problem there—a bright, bright kid, so freaked out by grade-level work that she just opts out?—then, I just . . . I don't even know where to start. It made no sense if, as the district claimed, everything was "just fine."

We tried everything to get Gracie back to school. But you can't just pick up a teenager and put her in the car, you know? We asked the district to work with us. We asked for help, believe me! I think their intentions may have been good, but they either had no idea how to aid us, or they were done with us. Whatever it was, they eventually reported us to the Truancy Office.

I still cannot believe they did that to us. We had to hire a lawyer—I think we've spent over sixty thousand dollars on legal and advocacy fees so far—and go to court to defend ourselves against these ridiculous truancy charges. Instead of working on solutions for healing our daughter and getting her back to school, we were forced to deal with a frightening legal situation.

The nightmare goes on and on from here. Long story short, after our first court date we were *finally* granted an IEP meeting, and then—a good *six years* after we'd begun advocating for special education services—Gracie went on an IEP. When she learned that she would have to attend a new school, a therapeutic day school, she had a psychiatric meltdown and ended up in the ER. After that it was the old story: school-refusal resumed, the truancy officer came back into our lives, and we were inches from losing custody of our girl, when all we'd done was try to get her help. . . . It was as if the school district didn't hear or understand anything we tried to tell them, and they misinterpreted every incident involving Gracie while she

---

YOU *CAN* BE YOUR KID'S SUPERHERO!

If one of the great barriers to appropriate, affordable mental health care for children in our society is the tyranny of the Bottom Line, there may not be much we, as individuals, can do besides advocate, inform, and keep the conversation going, loud and strong. But we *can* strengthen our personal odds of accessing the care our kids need and deserve by understanding the system as best we can and learning to communicate effectively with the folks who run it—from the gatekeepers to the people at the tippy-top. Sometimes that means "making nice" and ensuring you're well liked. In other cases, you'll need to be informed to the hilt and hard as steel, because making nice leads to people and systems abusing your trust. (In all honesty, most of us will face a learning curve before the distinction becomes readily apparent; good thing we've got lots of time ahead of us, for practice!) Educating yourself and others, including the people who work with your kid, learning when and how to listen, and when and how to use the most effective words, can mean the difference between your child languishing without proper treatment, and making forward progress. (As always, readers, your mileage may vary, but there's no doubt smart communication will give you an advantage.)

If getting up to speed sounds like a hellish amount of effort, it is—you're going to have to assess every situation, every relationship with the people and institutions your kid depends on and figure out the best approach to interacting with them. In the corporate world, this is sometimes described as "managing up"—that is, operating strategically to ensure you get the outcome you want without ruffling any feathers at the top or endangering your own position. Embrace the learning curve (if you can) as part of your growth into the job.

You may be in no shape, mentally or physically, to manage up. That's OK—you're far from alone! Basic survival always comes first. But keep in mind: you have more power than you think—even when it seems like the system has you beat.

was a public school student under their watch. Like, we came from different planets or something.

Where we are now, is homeschooling. We'd filed a homeschool plan before our last court date, and the family court judge dismissed the case. I think she realized it was ridiculous that two educated parents, who *wanted their kids to be in school*, had been brought before her.

When she dismissed the case, I broke down in front of everyone, I was hysterical. Hysterical.

I don't know if our family will ever get over this . . . and we have two younger kids in school here. I warn people all the time now. I tell them to be alert, to be persistent if they think their child needs accommodations or extra support. And to *never* let a teacher or administrator dismiss their concerns without taking them seriously.

I still don't know for sure why things went so badly amiss. I always took teachers and school staff at their word. I trusted them. Why wouldn't I? They go into teaching because they care about kids. I really do believe that. But now I see it's not so simple. If they say your kid is doing great, it could be true, or it could mean something else. Something they would never say aloud, like, "We're not allocating resources to *that* kid, even though she needs them." I bet they get away with that all the time—whatever their reason for doing it—because a lot of parents don't know how to fight it. Or even that there is anything to fight.

THE SECRET LIVES OF PATIENTS AND CLINICIANS, PART 2: MOMBOT, MEET DOCBOT

I've talked about the "MomBot" more than once in these pages. She's what I've named the part of me that rises out of the flames of crisis and just keeps going until the crisis is over. She's fueled by overcaffeination and sheer force of will. She survives by compartmentalizing, *doing*, and not thinking beyond the next task. She doesn't focus on the inner trauma, because to do so would be perilous. Sleep deprivation? Bone-weariness? Perpetual alertness to danger? Those things are nothing to the MomBot . . . but to me, the mom, they've been physically and mentally destructive. My inner MomBot has saved our family, more than once—but she's nearly killed me in the process.

It turns out our kids' mental health providers experience something similar, in their own instinctive responses to trauma and fear. And there's a growing recognition among practitioners that their profession, with its heavy reliance on emotional compartmentalization, and its systemic stigmatization of emotional display as weakness, needs some major reform. Well, there's a surprising but gratifying point of agreement between us: any parent of a psychiatrically disordered kid will tell you the system is broken!

Even more surprising, though, is this: the inner lives of parents and providers—cluttered with boxes and barriers for containing our anguish and separating it from our "working parts"—appear to have much in common.

Washington University Medical School psychiatrists Anne Glowinski and Dehra Harris have been mulling over this "DocBot" phenomenon. Privately, in conversation with me, Dr. Glowinski mentioned her concerns that the social stigma surrounding mental illness pervades even the ranks of psychiatrists—a situation she feels *must* change if patients are to receive the care they deserve, and if physicians are to care for their own mental and physical health.[3]

Here are Drs. Glowinski and Harris, writing on the subject of what the former has called, in response to my MomBot, the DocBot. I've included the full post here, with permission of the authors:

> We [physicians] have believed a lie to prop up an increasingly untenable system. We have behaved as if we could safely put our emotions aside to do our jobs at no substantial cost to ourselves in the process. We've all heard the admonishments.
>
> "I don't want my surgeon crying in the operating room. He needs to leave those emotions outside."
>
> Or: "This is just the way medicine is now. It has nothing to do with your feelings."
>
> Or: "Don't bring that 'stuff' home."
>
> We have been mentored by most of our role models to use a single tool for handling our emotions in medicine, and that is to compartmentalize them—to put them in a box, and get the job done. No one bothered to mention, probably because they too had been apprenticed that way into medicine, that there is no box big enough to practice medicine long term using just this tool and there is no way to put your emotions in a box without putting vital parts of yourself in there too.
>
> Now before you get worried that we are going to take your boxes away—we are not. We believe in compartmentalization. We have our own boxes, and we think they function very well . . . in the moment. That's the problem. We are using a coping skill that is designed for acute situations, and just because we have to use it over and over to survive, we think it can be used chronically. It cannot. Compartmentalization is something that works for short periods of hours to maximally days, but it is not a strategy that you can use exclusively for years without substantial cost. It does, however, reflect the natural outcome of a system that does not acknowledge rest, recovery or reintegration.

Let's walk through what happens when we compartmentalize. Compartmentalization is essentially a fancy form of denial, one that we begin using consciously but eventually, it becomes our default response. Emotions and responses are triggered by an event, and we train ourselves to become good at focusing on other cues and ignoring our emotions to concentrate on a crucial task at hand. No one can argue that this is not an absolutely vital skill during a crisis. Emotions are a high-energy endeavor and can bring up unwanted behaviors and responses without invoking the parts of our brain we typically use for higher order reasoning.

What happens after the crisis is over? What's the cost of compartmentalizing?

You can ask any physician you know about compartmentalization, and you will likely get a staunch defense of this process as necessary. I want you to ask a follow-up question. Ask them to tell you the story of the very first really disturbing thing they saw in medicine. Without exception, they have one. And it is highly likely you have never heard it unless you are a colleague or were there when it happened. This is the story that first started their complex relationship with compartmentalization. This is when they made the box where they started putting their stories of a broken system. When these boxes got full you started to see the symptoms of burnout: fatigue, illness, insomnia, worry, lack of empathy . . . because all the energy it takes to keep things in a box is eventually too much for anyone.

But don't stop there. The most telling question of all happens next. Ask them if anyone ever talked to them about that first broken story and helped them make sense of it and their role in medicine. A system that champions compartmentalization denies the reality of trauma—which is that our brain is exquisitely wired to vividly recall and respond to memories that have had a strong emotional charge with big responses. So we train new responses, but we cannot undo the wiring that registers this stress at the body level. No one ever helps them unpack the box and reintegrate into medicine, much less the rest of their life.

And where does this leave us? A very demoralized work force stuck in a perpetual loop of employing short-term coping strategies in pursuit of long term solutions. If you were going to design a tool that keeps people from rising up to challenge the system it would be hard to make a better one. After all, you can blame individuals who speak up about the emotional drain of their work and the lack of control they experience and say they are "not doing it right." Say they are "too emotional."

We are finally talking about burnout, but now it is time to take a deeper look into the emotional mechanisms that make it persist. Even if we have an emerging thoughtful national conversation about burnout, the culture of medicine as of now treats the symptoms of burnout as individual weaknesses. They are not. We can't seriously tell doctors to take better care of themselves within a system that does not care for them. Don't teach us to meditate when our practice of medicine will rapidly undo the benefits of meditation. Instead, sit down with us and have the hard conversations about a culture that is so toxic that it is breaking the physicians, nurses, and other health professionals who work in it. We cannot continue to compartmentalize. You cannot continue to blame us. Every case of burnout has to be seen for what it truly is: a system failure. And because of that, it is time [to] stop talking about small scale solutions and focus on the courage it takes to reform medicine, so that [it] is sustainable for the people who practice it.[4]

PARENT-PROFESSIONAL Q&A: KATE MAFFA, MENTAL HEALTH PARENT AND ACTIVIST, ANSWERS MY QUESTIONS ABOUT MAKING THE BEST OF A HEALTH CARE SYSTEM THAT'S NOT DESIGNED FOR OUR KIDS

DV: Kate, as parent of two kids with significant psychiatric illnesses and a long history of treatment and hospitalizations, what would you say are the strengths and the weaknesses of pediatric and adolescent mental health care in America?

KM: The list of positives is much shorter than the negatives. And it all differs from state to state, which is a serious problem, because it means there is no such thing as standard or equal mental health care for children living across the U.S.

I could go on forever about what is working and what is broken, but I'll focus on one Massachusetts program that has made a big difference in *my* family's life: the Children's Behavioral Health Initiative (CBHI). CBHI and other state-funded mental health programming came into being in response to a lawsuit, filed on behalf of a child who died of neglect and abuse because her case was not being managed closely through the Department of Children and Families (DCF) system. CBHI helps families access more appropriate, integrative care for children with complex issues. It also considers the child's issues in the context of the entire family, which is important. CBHI is an excellent starting point. I wish other states would adopt a similar model, so fewer kids living in the U.S. would fall through the cracks. Then we could continue the push forward from there.

My list of negatives: the system forces parents to hunt and peck for services, which tend to be siloed, with minimal intersection/communication between them. There is no way to access a comprehensive treatment program through a single resource center. And it can be very difficult to locate, apply, and get approved for services that do exist, because information is hard to find.

Then, of course, there's the stigma in our communities against people with behavioral and mental health challenges—clearly not limited to one part of the country. A long, convoluted pathway to accurate diagnosis and effective treatment. Families suffer, and too often, the message seems to be that the child is beyond help.

DV: How would you advise parents whose concerns are dismissed by school officials and health care professionals to tune out the noise and start the process of seeking appropriate services for their kids?

KM: Become the expert on your own child. Learn how to search for resources related to his or her specific needs. Talk to people, consult and reconsult with specialists, and especially find other families who've been through similar circumstances, to see how they manage.

The other critical component for staying focused and on track is to surround yourself with positive people who "get" you. That may be the most crucial part of this whole experience: finding the right support networks.

Finally, take it one day at a time. Tomorrow's another day.

DV: Name what you consider the two or three greatest specific barriers to accessing good and affordable mental health care, in your state and/or nationally.

KM: It's very difficult to find the right mental health clinicians. Not all of them are appropriate for all kids, and it can take cycling through several before you find the right fit. Also, most people are constrained by the limitations of their insurance. Here's another instance of unequal care . . . there's tremendous variation in coverage, locally and nationwide. If there were a universal standard of care, it would make a big difference in terms of the suffering kids and families endure.

Last, mental health disorders are still not widely thought of as "equal" to medical illnesses, so children and families receive unequal access to treatment based on the nature of their illness.

DV: What do you think needs to change if children with mental illnesses are to receive treatment and care commensurate with that which medically ill kids currently receive?

KM: We need to accept that mental health disorders are brain-based disorders, and not a matter of choice or bad decisions. Everyone is affected when mental health care is substandard: our neighborhoods, towns, states, and ultimately the entire country.

DV: How can readers who want to make a positive impact on a larger scale, like you are doing, get started?

KM: Try to network with any organization involved with treatment and care of children, whether it be a medical center program for children's behavioral health, or a national or state organization, such as the National Alliance on Mental Illness (NAMI). Start with an internet search and go from there.[5]

CHILD-TO-PARENT VIOLENCE IS REAL—
BUT GETTING HELP CAN BE HARD: TINA'S STORY

Tina, a single mom from northern Connecticut, has one child—a teenage daughter with schizophrenia and a history of violence, primarily against Tina herself. I asked her to describe what it's like to seek help, when confusion and stigma surround all kinds of mental illness, but especially when violence is involved—and what she thinks could be the key to families like hers being heard and understood.

Tina: It's often the people who are supposed to help that hurt us the most. Here in Connecticut, we have relatively decent mental health services, and you can have your kid evaluated at home by a mobile crisis team if he or she is unstable. These people are generally social workers, and, one would hope, well trained in assessing crisis situations and making hospital referrals.

So, my daughter's violent, and has been for a long time. It's scary, being attacked by your own child, and it gets scarier as she gets bigger. One time, when she was about twelve, I called the crisis team hoping they'd come to the house and refer her to hospital admission. After listening to our story, observing my kid, and taking stock of the situation, the senior clinician said, "Since you've been hit and kicked by your daughter on a regular basis for at least a couple of years, we would consider this to be the 'baseline' for your household. Unfortunately, that means you would not be eligible for any interventions at this time."

I was stunned. That logic was ridiculous! What—I'd survived the physical abuse for so long it was no longer abuse? Are you *kidding me*? I thought, *Who is this person, who's making determinations about interventions and can't understand, on a basic level, what is wrong with this picture?*

I said to the crisis team leader, "Are you telling me we can't have assistance because the abuse is *normal* for us?"

"That's right," she said.

Well, that felt like another punch and kick, only from the person I thought was going to protect me, and help me get acute treatment for my child.

I am so glad our in-home therapist was present at the time, because she was able to make things right. She called the agency and spoke directly to that person's clinical supervisor. Eventually, we got my daughter into the hospital. That was already her fourth or fifth hospitalization, by the way (we're up to nine, now, but I'm not counting anymore).

One thing that actually helped in terms of dealing with the ignorance and victim blaming—it's incredible, how many people will tell you what you're doing wrong if you make the mistake of opening up to them—was when my daughter finally got a concrete diagnosis of schizophrenia.

Previous to that, she'd had been diagnosed with everything, you know, all over the map. I remember seeing a behavioral pediatrician around that time, who could only describe her as "complex." We'd go see Specialist A, and they'd say, "Oh, she's definitely 'my type of patient,'" and if we went to Specialist B, they'd say, "Oh, no, I'm convinced she's this other thing," and so on. We saw countless specialists before anyone figured out what was going on there.

Actually, the way my daughter was finally diagnosed was through a research study. That was so worth doing! They spent at least ten clinical hours with her, conducting all kinds of tests and interviews, and interviews with me too. At the end of it, they gave me a report (printed on their letterhead, which meant something because this was a prestigious hospital), which said she was "at high clinical risk for psychosis."

Once we had that report in hand, clinicians sat up and listened. Most of them did.

I always advise other parents of complex kids to try and participate in a research study—the depth of information you'll receive, and connections to resources you might otherwise never know about, are incredibly worthwhile. And doing it will cost you nothing! You will probably even receive a stipend and parking or transportation reimbursement, which helps for people on a tight budget.

I guess the conclusion to be drawn from our story, is—well, there's probably a negative one and a positive one. The world still has *so far to go*, in terms of public and professional education about mental illnesses, and access to appropriate interventions. I mean, at one hospital, a worker actually told my daughter she wasn't schizophrenic. Nope. *You're possessed by Satan!* she said. So, yeah.

On the other hand, once there was more diagnostic clarity, things did get better, overall. Not totally great, though. We will always be living with this illness, and I have no idea what the future holds for my girl—or me, for that matter. We just do a lot of finger crossing around here.

RESOURCES FOR READING, LISTENING, AND VIEWING

- Dr. Ross Greene, author of the iconic book *The Explosive Child* and a tireless advocate for our kids, has a website, Lives in the Balance, filled with multimedia resources for parents of behaviorally difficult kids: https://www.livesinthebalance.org/. Don't miss this one!
- If you're interested in reading what current research says about barriers to aid and treatment, especially if your child is violent, check out "Mothers of Violent Children with Mental Illness: How They Perceive Barriers to Effective Help," by Karyn Sporer and Dana L. Radatz: https://umaine.edu/sociology/wp-content/uploads/sites/55/2017/08/Sporer-Radatz-Mothers-Barriers.pdf.
- Want to participate in a clinical trial? Find one at the National Institute of Mental Health (NIMH) clinical trials database: https://www.nimh.nih.gov/health/trials/index.shtml.
- The blog *Bounceback Parenting* (https://bouncebackparenting.com/) is filled with great ideas and stories you'll immediately relate to, from real parents. The post "9 Tips for Parenting an Explosive Kid," by Shawn Fink, is particularly insightful—and practical! https://bouncebackparenting.com/9-tips-for-parenting-an-explosive-kid/.

NO CHILD IS AN ISLAND: OUR STORY, SNAPSHOT #14

The one aspect of being a human in a sea of humanity that gives me the most trouble is putting myself first. Because, no matter how bad I've got it, there's someone else who's got it worse. Who am I to worry about the fact that I haven't had a real day off in ten years? Some people don't get to *live* ten years! Some spend more than ten years unfairly incarcerated, or dying slowly, or chronically hungry.

Same goes for the people in my life. I really, really want to gift myself a visit to a spa, but Saskia and Ben have never been to Disney World, which is really sad! And there's a chance to make it up to them (kind of), by taking that money I'd half considered spending on myself and using it on passes to Six Flags. You know the deal.

Either I inherited this stupid selflessness gene from my mom, or I learned the behavior from reading Victorian novels. (Victorian women, of most walks of life, came pretty much last—and I love me my Victorian novels.)

You can imagine how the selfless gene, plus the anxious gene, plus the gene of wild imagination, combined with a dear child who is always unsettled and wracked with anguish might cause some problems. And not just for me.

It was my job, as my mother's daughter and a devotee of Victorian fiction, to make sure my kids were happy and healthy, my husband was tended to, the cats and dogs and hermit crabs were talked to and watered and fed, before I got busy with myself. If they weren't, I had to do better.

For a long time, it was clear to me that none of us four was OK, but I pretended it wasn't even a teensy bit translucent. We were all anxious and depressed, but only in Ben did these feelings show themselves unambiguously. In Lars, the dysregulation emerged as anger; I knew better than to poke at *that* dragon with suggestions of getting some psychiatric help. I just nurtured and flinched and forgave as well as I could. In Saskia, the off-kilter emotions looked like silence, a need for intense privacy, a preference for hanging out at friends' houses (and for her friends' parents), and occasional reminders that she really, truly hated our guts.

In me? Oh, the MomBot took care of *that*. She made the trauma in me look like industriousness, intense focus, impatience, bursts of energy (fueled by caffeine and terror, only you'd never have known it from the outside), and an unsmiling demeanor. No time to stop and think about *my* health! Lars is an adult; he can wait a little for his care. Saskia? Oh, she's *fine*! She's over at Leela's house tonight. I *totally* believe her when she says she's fine, because why would she lie about something like anxiety or depression? Hey, we *do* depression and anxiety around here. She knows that. It would be no problem at all if she came forward with a mental illness, although she hasn't. Yup, that's what Mom's here for!

The MomBot was superhelpful in these regards: she kept me on the ready for every single Benjy crisis—the expected and the unannounced—and she allowed me to sustain the lie that three other people in our household were doing great. That was one important lie, because even the MomBot would have been no match for Benjy plus two others and me.

It's crazy how invested we can be (we human beings, I mean) in misreading the unspoken signals other people are sending us—the emotional

Morse code that all of us employ, when parts of our inner chaos can't be verbalized but need to be noticed. Sometimes, what we really need if we're to deal with the emotional pain swelling under the surface, is permission to name it, and do something about it.

Benjy was the only one of us four who'd found a way to ask permission. And Benjy was receiving all the help we could find him—thank goodness!

An attending physician in the pediatric psych unit where Benjy was a repeat customer through age twelve was only the second person to ever accurately read my emotional Morse code at a time of severe crisis. (The first was Dr. Leon Hammer, whom you may have met in a snapshot in the opening chapter of this book.) Ben's doctor gave me permission to work on healing myself, and to help my husband and daughter to do the same. It happened in a most unlikely way.

Lars and I had given up resisting the idea of a residential school for Ben. We were nearing the point of surrender. We were just a family, after all. We would never have several mental health staff always on duty at home, 24/7, or the firm structure of the psych unit. We could not provide our child the right kind of peers or pull him some friends out of thin air. It took us years to get there, but we were finally ready to admit it.

At an IEP meeting in the hospital, we discussed with his clinical/ educational team how a residential school might provide him just those things—and by doing so, maybe save his life.

He was not yet thirteen years old, and he'd already been many times to hell and back. I *wanted* to send him to boarding school, because some days I thought I might be dying. But I was paralyzed with fear that sending him away might kill the two of us.

So, we sat around the conference table in an institutional-looking hospital room that should have seemed sad but was kind of a second home to us. I must have been looking entreatingly at the doctor, face and hands working as they tend to do when I'm strung out on cortisol, because he turned to me suddenly and said, in a low, compassionate voice, "You know, no child lives in a vacuum. There are others in your home who need and deserve some care."

I don't remember if I cried just then. I know I did for days and weeks after, alternating between tears of relief and sobs of anguish. For years, I had all this dysfunction inside me, and I'd repressed and despised and denied it. And here was this psychiatrist, a good man with no real personal stake in our lives, but, I suppose, a generous impulse to heal, opening a path for me, for us, to self-care.

It was only the second time I'd had a silent plea answered so perfectly, with such empathy, clarity, and kindness. I'm sure it hasn't happened since, but at least I know better, now, how to do this mental health stuff.

THE TAKEAWAY

- You can be, and should be, a partner in your child's mental health care.
- No one is as qualified as you are to be your kid's parent-professional; your knowledge of his or her thoughts, behaviors, triggers, and needs is second to none.
- By improving your communications skills by practicing empathy and situational intelligence, you may find ways to topple some of the common barriers to support and care.
- Ignorance and disinformation about childhood mental illnesses abound. If you *can* speak publicly about kids and mental health disorders, do it—loud, often, and true.
- You *can* learn how to understand, and interact with, the gatekeepers to resources and care in ways that make it easier to get through the "gate." Again, use your situational intelligence to read between the lines.
- Know when to fight and when to withdraw—and how best to retreat so you can return with a friend, a social worker, an advocate, a fellow parent . . . or anyone who can play your "good cop" or "bad cop" and help you achieve your goal.
- As with every suggestion offered to you in this book, your mileage may vary. This is all about trying, failing, trying again, seeking advice, accepting and offering help, and never, ever giving up on your child. *You got this, parent-warriors!* And the Rest of Us have got your back.

AFTERWORD

MOVING FORWARD

One night, when my kids were eleven and thirteen, I woke from a fretful sleep and got up to use the toilet. Out of habit, I glanced in my son's room as I padded quietly down the hall toward the bathroom. I noticed the usual moonlit shapes, eerily still—dresser, desk, rumpled bed, toys and clothes on the floor. My brain didn't register the absence of a person in there until I'd turned away. Then, a moment of wild terror. I gasped violently, bent over with one hand pressed against my thudding heart, the other hand braced on my knee. I stayed that way until I caught my breath, whispering, "He's alive, he's safe," again and again, as if those four small words had magic powers.

We had left him, a few hours earlier, at the hospital for his first inpatient psychiatric admission. I have not yet found words to convey the misery of that good-bye, so I'll just let you imagine. Benjy, for his part, seemed to understand he had to live at the hospital for a while, if he wanted to keep on living—though that didn't stop him from changing his mind at the last minute. When he realized his pleas to be sprung from that place were useless, he sobbed and hung on to me, his truest lifeline.

"Don't ever forget me," he begged as we were escorted out by a very nice young mental health counselor.

No one died that night, but twice (at least) I thought I would. The first time was when Lars and I shuffled away from our sobbing child. The second? Later that night, when I looked in his bedroom, and saw there was no boy in there.

No one signs up for this way of life. No parent, no child, no person of any age who dwells in the off-kilter zone that is mental illness. Even so, those of us who find ourselves there can—and must—make our peace with it. If we believe that "normal" is a myth and accept that *our* normal may be hard, but is neither wrong nor broken, we can often move ahead with the business of living.

Right now, "moving ahead with the business of living" may read, to you, like a cruel joke. How are you ever going to get there from here? I can't tell you how, exactly, except you will use your reserves of courage, energy, and love, become a MomBot or DadBot if you must, hoist your emotional shield and press forward, doing what it takes—until someday, you find yourself in a better place.

There's no knowing when it's going to happen—and unfortunately, no firm guarantee that it will. But here's the thing: it *can* happen. You can, with the help of your family, parent networks, some good clinicians and educators, get to a place where life is easier. Where you allow yourself to look hopefully, even confidently, to the future. Just remind yourself, whenever you can, that the hour-to-hour, day-to-day way you approach life now may not be permanent. Act as if it won't be. Keep doing what you can for your child (stopping, when possible, for a self-care break), because the future matters—even when you can't conceive of what that future holds.

The reason I was able to write this book at all is that *we got there*. When my family was able to imagine the horizon, and I believed in my heart that Ben would not only live, but thrive, I finally moved beyond survival mode and had the capacity to embark on other things.

Our son will always have bipolar disorder. He will always have anxiety and some specific learning disabilities. He'll always be prone to cognitive distortion, rigid thinking. His risk for suicide, self-harm, and all the other challenges that come with his diagnoses are never going away. But he's learning to manage them. And these issues no longer eclipse his intelligence, his kindness, his desire to do well, and do lots and lots of good. He's funny. He's interesting. A joy to spend time with. His emotional flares are much shorter in duration and more easily contained. He has learned what he needs to do to reset his moods.

I mentioned that I've moved on to other things. That's true, but a bit misleading. There's never a day—an hour, really—that doesn't find me thinking about both my kids and hoping they're holding strong. I'm still here, ready and waiting to be called back to the front line. It happens now and then. I'm mostly prepared.

OK. So, what next? You've read this book. Your kid is still deeply emotionally impaired. Life continues to be hugely challenging, although I hope you've found some new, useful strategies and a sense of camaraderie with other parents like you. School continues to be a day-by-day experiment, diagnoses continue to blindside you, and you may still be using fast food or other awful bribes to get your kid from here to there.

If there's one thing you can do besides hold it together and keep your family safe, fed, clothed, and on their feet, let it be to *talk*. Do so in spoken words, emails, essays, letters, social media posts. Tell the true story of childhood mental illness, every chance you get. Blow a hole in the false narratives about mental health disorders. Educate, inform, refuse to be a bystander.

But only do these things when there's enough oxygen in your atmosphere, a clear space in your brain, and time on your side. Because the business of shepherding your family and yourself safely forward in the world comes first.

Readers? We have the potential to be a mighty force for good. It won't be easy. The structural problems in our mental health care system are way bigger than we are. Still, singly and collectively, we can spread awareness that childhood mental illnesses have reached "epidemic" proportion. That *all* of us are affected by untreated/unacknowledged psychiatric illnesses in our communities. We can expose widespread stigma when and where we encounter it, and comment on inequities in funding and available treatments for mental versus bodily illnesses.

Practice empathy, let go of your old expectations, and embrace the child you have. Work not to change him, but to make his life better—more sustainable, satisfying, and productive. Help her live her life—the one she *wants* to live and can.

Together we can do this! We are champions, unacknowledged but fierce.

NOTES

CHAPTER 1

1. "Mental Health by the Numbers," National Alliance on Mental Illness, https://www.nami.org/Learn-More/Mental-Health-By-the-Numbers.

2. For example: Bipolar disorder. Borderline personality disorder. Panic disorder. Obsessive compulsive disorder. Major depressive disorder. Trichotillomania. Psychotic disorder. Schizophrenia. Oppositional defiant disorder. Reactive attachment disorder. For more information on diagnoses, treatments, statistics, and so on, visit the National Institute of Mental Health (NIMH): https://www.nimh.nih.gov/index.shtml. Or, if you're feeling ambitious, check out the American Psychiatric Association's *DSM-5: Diagnostic and Statistical Manual of Mental Disorders*, 5th ed. (Washington, DC: American Psychiatric Association, 2013).

3. Interview with Jessica Reed, LICSW, by author, March 2017.

CHAPTER 2

1. Stephanie Castillo, "The Happiness Trick You Haven't Tried," *Prevention*, November 21, 2012, http://www.prevention.com/mind-body/emotional-health/dancing-shown-help-boost-happiness-and-mental-health.

2. Amy Novotney, "Music as Medicine," *Monitor on Psychology* 44, no. 10 (November 2013), http://www.apa.org/monitor/2013/11/music.aspx.

3. "Teen Brain Less Discerning of Threat vs. Safety, More Vulnerable to Stress," National Institute of Mental Health, April 28, 2011, https://www.nimh.nih.gov/news/science-news/2011/teen-brain-less-discerning-of-threat-vs-safety-more-vulnerable-to-stress.shtml.

4. Mandy Oaklander, "Science Says Your Pet Is Good for Your Mental Health," *Time Health*, April 6, 2017, http://time.com/4728315/science-says-pet-good-for-mental-health/.

CHAPTER 3

1. Donna Hardaker, "Speaking Up for a New Normal," *National Post Canada*, Mental Health and Wellness Supplement by MediaPlanet, May 2011.

2. "How to File an ADA Complaint with the U.S. Department of Justice," ADA.gov, https://www.ada.gov/filing_complaint.htm.

CHAPTER 4

1. "Mental Illness," National Institute of Mental Health, last updated November 2017, https://www.nimh.nih.gov/health/statistics/prevalence/any-disorder-among -children.shtml.

2. In the U.S., all students with disabilities are entitled to equal access (as mandated in the Americans with Disabilities Act [ADA]) and a free and appropriate public education, per the Individuals with Disabilities Education Act (IDEA).

3. The American Psychological Association offers a concise, readable summary of IDEA on its website: http://www.apa.org/advocacy/education/idea/index.aspx.

4. Interview with Cynthia Moore, Massachusetts-based special education advocate/activist, by author, November 2017.

5. "Is Corporal Punishment an Option in Your State?" *Education Week*, August 23, 2016, https://www.edweek.org/ew/section/multimedia/states-ban-corporal -punishment.html; published in print as "Where Schools Use Corporal Punishment, " *Education Week* 36, no. 1 (2016): 18.

6. Interview with Cynthia Moore, November 2017.

CHAPTER 5

1. Judith E. Glaser, "Listen to Connect: Miracles Happen When We Do," posted on Glaser's *Conversational Intelligence* blog, PsychologyToday.com, December 23, 2017, https://www.psychologytoday.com/blog/conversational-intelligence/201712/ listen-connect.

CHAPTER 6

1. Dr. Leon Hammer, from a personal correspondence with the author, October, 2017.

2. Audrey Nath, "A Physician Lurked on Facebook Mom Groups. Here's What She Found," *KevinMD* (blog), January 9, 2018.

3. Anne Glowinski, private email conversation with the author, January 2018.

4. Dehra Harris and Anne Glowinski, "The Deception at the Heart of Physician Burnout," *KevinMD* (blog), August 31, 2017.

5. Interview with Kate Maffa by author, January 2018. Kate Maffa is a mental health parent and activist in Massachusetts.

BIBLIOGRAPHY

Selected Reading and Resources, for When You Can

BOOKS

American Psychiatric Association. *Diagnostic and Statistical Manual of Mental Disorders*. 5th ed. Washington, DC: American Psychiatric Association, 2013.

Davenport, Randi. *The Boy Who Loved Tornadoes*. Chapel Hill, NC: Algonquin Books of Chapel Hill, 2010.

Gallagher, Gina, and Patricia Konjoian. *Shut Up about Your Perfect Kid: A Survival Guide for Ordinary Parents of Special Children*. New York: Three Rivers, 2010.

Greene, Ross W. *The Explosive Child: A New Approach for Understanding and Parenting Easily Frustrated, Chronically Inflexible Children*. New York: Harper Paperbacks, 1998.

Long, Liza, and Karen White. *The Price of Silence: A Mom's Perspective on Mental Illness*. New York: Avery, 2014.

Miklowitz, David J., and Elizabeth L. George. *The Bipolar Teen: What You Can Do to Help Your Child and Family*. New York: Guilford, 2007.

Shapiro, Lawrence E., and Robin K. Sprague. *The Relaxation and Stress Reduction Workbook for Kids: Help for Children to Cope with Stress, Anxiety, and Transitions*. New York: New Harbinger, 2009.

Solomon, Andrew. *Far from the Tree: Parents, Children and the Search for Identity*. New York: Scribner, 2012.

———. *The Noonday Demon: An Atlas of Depression*. New York: Scribner, 2001.

BLOGS

A Day in Our Shoes: IEP Resources, Support and More from a Special Needs Mom and Advocate. https://www.adayinourshoes.com/.

Blue Light Blue: Living through Mental Illness. http://www.bluelightblue.com/.

Bounceback Parenting. https://www.bouncebackparenting.com/.

KevinMD. https://www.kevinmd.com/blog/.

Psychology Today. https://www.psychologytoday.com/.

Storied Mind: Recover Life from Depression. https://www.storiedmind.com/.

The Striped Nickel; or, What to Expect When You Get the Unexpected. http://www
.thestripednickel.blogspot.com.

Vlock, Deborah. *What to Expect When You Get the Unexpected: A Mother's Notes on
Childhood Mental Illness. Psychology Today.* https://www.psychologytoday.com/
blog/what-expect-when-you-get-the-unexpected.

WEBSITES

Advocate Tip of the Day (Cynthia Moore). https://m.facebook.com/AdvocateTip
oftheDay/.

Federation for Children with Special Needs. https://www.fcsn.org/.

Hardaker, Donna. http://www.donnahardaker.com/.

Lives in the Balance. https://www.livesinthebalance.org/.

National Association of Parents with Children in Special Education. http://www
.napcse.org/.

National Council on Independent Living. https://www.ncil.org/.

Wrightslaw Special Education Rights and Advocacy. http://www.wrightslaw.com.

GOVERNMENT AGENCIES

National Institute of Mental Health. https://www.nimh.nih.gov/index.shtml.

———. "Clinical Trials: Information for Participants." https://www.nimh.nih
.gov/health/trials/index.shtml.

U.S. Department of Education. https://www.ed.gov/.

U.S. Department of Justice Civil Rights Division. "Information and Technical
Assistance on the Americans with Disabilities Act." https://www.ada.gov/
taprog.htm.

U.S. Department of Labor. "Family and Medical Leave Act." https://www.dol
.gov/whd/fmla/.

INDEX

Note: all single first names are fictitious.

ABOUT THE AUTHOR

Deborah Vlock frequently writes about the impact of disability and mental health disorders on families. She uses her writing as one means of promoting constructive dialogue on mental health issues—primarily from a parent's perspective. Deborah has a PhD in English literature from Brandeis University and in her past life was an academic, publishing a number of scholarly articles and a monograph on Charles Dickens (*Dickens, Novel Reading, and the Victorian Popular Theatre*, 1998). Her essays and short stories have appeared in glossy magazines, literary journals, and online media. She's a sometime blogger on the tricky balancing act of living life as fully as possible while parenting complex kids. You can find her posts on her *Psychology Today* blog, *A Mother's Notes on Childhood Mental Illness* (https://www.psychologytoday.com/blog/what-expect-when-you-get-the-unexpected), as well as *The Striped Nickel* (www.thestripednickel.blogspot.com).

Deborah has been invited to present on the subject of mental health parenting at hospital grand rounds and to lend trainees in pediatric psychiatry a parent's perspective. She also is actively involved in special education parent groups, where she offers (and gratefully accepts) insights, suggestions, solidarity, and hope. Her best and most fulfilling roles, though, will always be mother to "Saskia" and "Ben," wife to "Lars," devoted daughter, and indulger in chief of household pets. You can connect with Deb, and read her published work, at www.deborahvlock.com.